(1988)

£2-50

Ge

9/51

THE EUROPEAN OPEN

THE FIRST TEN YEARS

Panasonic European Open

THE EUROPEAN OPEN

THE FIRST TEN YEARS

edited by

RENTON LAIDLAW

BIRCHGREY LTD
Sporting Promotions

The Editor wishes to thank the following:
Tony Jacklin for writing the Foreword.
Bob Brand, Managing Director of *Golf Illustrated* for his permission
to use material first published in *Golf Illustrated*.
Ken Schofield, Director of the European Tour.
Richard Dewing, Managing Director of Sports Editions.
David Cannon, Director of Allsport.
Nicholas Winton of Garrard, Crown Jewellers.
Keith Almond, Secretary, Sunningdale Golf Club.
The Directors of Birchgrey Ltd.

SPORTS EDITIONS LTD
Art Director
Mary Hamlyn
Design Assistants
Adrian Waddington
Sandra Cowell
Editor
Geraldine Christy

First published in 1988 by Birchgrey Ltd
Distributed by The Arena Press
Russell Chambers, The Piazza,
Covent Garden, London WC2 8AA

Copyright © 1988 Sports Editions

ISBN 1-85443-010-6

Produced, edited and designed by Sports Editions, 3 Greenlea Park,
Prince George's Road, London SW19 2JD

Typeset by Typesmiths, London.
Origination by APG Photolitho, Stockport.
Printed in Great Britain by
Purnell Book Production Limited
Member of the BPCC Group

Contents

As Ryder Cup captain for the past three matches I am only too well aware of the task of welding together into a winning unit golfers of various nationalities with just one common aim - to beat the Americans.

We have done so in the last two matches and we came desperately close to winning in the 1983 fixture in Florida but my point is a simple one. Europeans can work well together. Golf, in this respect, has been a Common Market now for quite some time.

I am a committed European - most certainly English and British - but European too and in this respect the growth of our circuit and the huge success of the Panasonic European Open - the event which encapsulates the idea of togetherness - pleases me no end.

You see I was in at the start. The then chief executive of the Tour John Jacobs, with a little help from me along the way, was instrumental in broadening the whole base of tournament golf in the early 70s. The cosy British circuit was replaced by a vibrant new circuit embracing all the leading countries in Europe.

It was a time of great diplomacy. No Continental Federation likes their authority eroded in any way. The negotiations needed to be handled by men with tact but with a firmness of purpose that would keep the project on the right path. In John Jacobs and later Ken Schofield the Tour was fortunate in its choice of leader. Both men believed in the principle of a European family of golfing nations and that is what we have today with the European Open the flagship of the integrated circuit.

There were growing pains with this championship, the brainchild of my friend from Stockholm Sven Tumba. He launched it, but the mechanics of running a multi-sponsored event took its financial toll and the project we all wanted to succeed was sinking slowly towards oblivion in 1981 when another friend of European golf came along to save the day.

Peter Urwin, who underwrote a Tour bond and later, with three original sponsors who had had their fingers burned, set up the Birchgrey company to ensure the future profitability of the financially unstable event, took a calculated gamble in 1981 - a gamble he was prepared to take because of the respect in which he held Ken Schofield and his Wentworth team.

Now firmly established the event mirrors what is happening in

Europe. The game, helped massively by the swashbuckling performances over the years of a man I much admire, Severiano Ballesteros, is in great heart. So too is the European Open. Significantly, Ballesteros has never won it although he has played each year. He has come close and will win sooner rather than later because it is a title, as Tumba predicted, that means so very much.

Along with the Open, the PGA Championship and the Irish Open it comprises a leg of what might be called our European Grand Slam. None of the current top five in Europe have won all four titles. Seve is missing the European, Lyle the Irish, Faldo the Irish and the European, Langer the Open and Woosnam has won only one of them - the PGA and that was at Wentworth in 1988. The fact that the event is always played on recognised championship courses is another reason why the tournament attracts probably the strongest field outside the Open. Just ten years into what is going to be a tremendous long-term future for the tournament it has a reputation world-wide others envy.

There have been, since 1978, two American winners. Two Australians have taken the title, and a Japanese has also landed a first prize cheque. The five Europeans who have been successful - Paul Way, Manuel Pinero, Sandy Lyle, Bernhard Langer and Gordon Brand junior - have all been, or are members of, my Ryder Cup squad in recent years. That gives me great pleasure too.

If John Jacobs and I tended to underestimate the potential of the European Tour when we began the big adventure eighteen years or so ago, I am in no doubt at all now that the liveliest of the four world circuits is ready for even further growth and greater personal successes from an even larger pool of world-class international golfing jet-setters who will keep coming back to play in the Championship with a title everyone wants to win - the European Open.

There is tremendous prestige for any player in being able to claim by right that he is European Champion. It is amazing to think that it is only ten years old. Its reputation has grown faster than any other event I can recall.

To all associated with the stylish staging of the Championship each year, to all the sponsors who make it possible, to the fans who add so much atmosphere and to the players who get excited by it and produce some of the finest golf imaginable during the four rounds - continued success.

Tony Jacklin
Ryder Cup Captain

Ken Schofield, Executive Director of the PGA European Tour.

Tom Watson wins the 1977 Open Championship at Turnberry, venue for the 1979 European Open, by one shot in a dramatic shoot-out with Jack Nicklaus.

The European Open Golf Championship is, by title and definition, a special event. It has a unique place in my mind, both professionally and personally, because of the circumstances surrounding its conception by Sven Tumba and because of the sometimes difficult financial sponsorship requirements in the early years. For me, the European Open really began at the 1977 Ryder Cup match at Royal Lytham and St Anne's when Sven Tumba's idea to stage such a championship in England, without obtaining the backing of a major sponsor, was convincing enough to myself and a number of my senior colleagues, and subsequently the Tournament Committee of that year, for us to give the project the green light.

For the next six months I spent much time, mostly with George O'Grady, attending various meetings in and around London, first to ensure a suitable venue and a suitable television contract and then – along with Sven's appointed tournament organisers, Executive Sports Inc. (the golf group from Florida in which Jack Nicklaus was involved), to make all the necessary arrangements for the proper staging of the championship.

Walton Heath, as a London championship course, was at the top of our priority list and although our friends there, led by the very fine Secretary, Bill McCrea, were slightly concerned because of the very late autumn date, agreement was fairly quickly reached.

Sven Tumba had in mind the European Open starting and remaining a "clean" title. His idea was to have many companies involved as sponsors but without any head sponsor's name appearing in the title. This, certainly for a British Isles based tournament, was a startling innovation. Until the arrival of the 1978 European Open, the traditional British sponsored events had had one main sponsor who normally picked up all the bills – or most of them – in exchange for having all the promotional visibility and, in many cases, control of virtually all areas of the tournament, save for those directly under the PGA European Tour's control. It took some time for this new European Open idea to be accepted by potential sponsors and, in the first year, a tremendous amount of start-up costs were also encountered, but the championship was staged and was, unquestionably, a sporting success.

The second year of the European Open brought more changes. Turnberry in Scotland was chosen as the 1979 venue following the most spectacular 1977 Open Championship there won by Tom Watson but the commercial and financial side of the championship remained a problem. In September 1980, the championship returned to Walton Heath and although first-class efforts were made by all concerned, the event did not – as is so often the case – recapture the sporting drama and feeling of the initial 1978 tournament.

Sven Tumba, whose vision and determination was responsible for the birth of the European Open.

Three tournaments had now been staged, but not many weeks later, on returning from a visit to Australia, I learned from Bill McCrea that, perhaps, all was not as well as we had thought regarding the tournament's financial affairs. The remaining months of the 1980-81 winter from mid-November were dire days indeed for what is now one of our flagship events. Sven Tumba tried with all his might and main to rescue the event and, although he himself became detached from the day-to-day organisation and a new company was set up specially to take the tournament forward into 1981, he did introduce a number of Scandinavian-based companies whose support at that time, and, still today, remain most valued. Sven's tremendous personality and drive played a large part in saving his idea and perhaps this would be the appropriate moment for me to pay tribute to his vision and integrity.

By April 1981, a new Board with fresh capital had emerged and, although we were not to know it, the arrival of Birchgrey at that time was to prove most inspired. I feel very proud of the efforts of our office staff during those difficult winter days before Easter 1981 and the enormous contribution made by my secretary, Marina Bray. Perhaps our lowest moment was an appearance at the Swedish Trade Embassy in London to explain to many companies, large and not so large, who had provided genuine service to the 1980 event, why their bills had not been completely paid six months or so after the tournament. In general terms the service companies in our golf industry have always proved most sympathetic to any local problems in cashflow and once we had the opportunity to explain that a fresh company was going to take over and maintain the entire integrity of the championship, we had enormous co-operation from virtually every quarter.

The 1981 event had, under the previous organisers, already been contracted to be played at Hoylake, home of the famous Royal Liverpool Golf Club so that was no problem but there were difficulties of another nature for the Tour that summer. A major and unfortunate appearance-money dispute with Severiano Ballesteros's then manager, Ed Barner, was virtually running parallel with the problems of the European Open and for most of 1981, Severiano's appearances in Europe were restricted and in Britain, non-existent. Perhaps fortuitously and certainly in what turned out to be a happy omen for the European Open and I believe, too, for Severiano, the Spaniard made his "come-back" appearance at Hoylake and came within a whisker of winning, leading well into the last round, only to be overtaken by the steady and indeed brilliant play of the great Australian Graham Marsh. Importantly the championship was again a sporting success.

Immediately at the conclusion of the Hoylake European Open I had been asked by Birchgrey, who wanted the event to return to London, to see

Severiano Ballesteros, whose association with the European open has been chequered - so far it is one of the titles that has eluded him.

David Cannon

Graham Marsh, who beat Ballesteros to the 1981 title at Hoylake.

Introduction

The Sunningdale clubhouse with the magnificent oak, the club's symbol, standing guard.

whether Sunningdale would be interested in taking the event on a more long-standing basis. I immediately contacted the late Gerald Micklem and, with his support, spoke to Keith Almond, the club secretary. Very quickly we reached the agreement Birchgrey wanted.

Peter Urwin, Managing Director of Birchgrey, with Isao Aoki, winner of the 1983 European Open at Sunningdale.

The 1982 Championship at Sunningdale, its home for the next five years and now in alternate years, was, of course, an outstanding success, as indeed all the European Opens have been over the famous course. Many of London's City-based companies were quick to respond to the personal and well co-ordinated marketing package put together initially by Birchgrey and later by their specially formed promotional company, Vantage Promotions.

The future of the Championship was further secured when, in 1983, Panasonic came on board as the main title sponsor, bringing to the event all their considerable international resources and skills. It has indeed proved to be a happy marriage. The many successes of the European Open since 1982 and the virtual parallel running growth between the Tour generally and the European Open can by no means be coincidental.

I would like to pay tribute to everyone who has contributed in whatever form to the success story - none more so than Birchgrey's Managing Director, Peter Urwin. His involvement has been central to the happy events of the last seven years from his initial role as PGA Tour "confidence broker" when he was prepared to invest in the event, to the point, today, when he has overall responsibility for the Championship. Thank you, Peter, for supporting myself, the Tour and what is now one of the world's great championships. May the next ten years continue to be very successful.

The Trophy

The challenge that faces any designer of a golf trophy is always the same – how to find a format that is not only unique but also pleasing to the eye. Alex Styles, (top designer for many of the 40 years he served with Garrard, the Crown jewellers in Regent Street), got it absolutely right when he designed the highly distinctive European Open Trophy. He sought to bring together the golfing nations of Europe in one unusual design and the European Open sponsors were delighted when he unveiled his masterpiece in early 1978, a few months before the first tournament.

There had been discussions, of course, and artists' impressions had been passed around but it was not until Alex Styles, now retired, produced the actual trophy that the promoters fully appreciated its beauty of line and the undeniable message it portayed of togetherness. Each participating nation's flag is enamelled on to the body of the trophy and, with shrewd forward planning, there are additional blank panels available for any other countries that may join in.

London has long been an important centre for the skilled craftsman in gold and silver. Alex Styles, during his career,

designed more hand-made silver than anyone else alive. He had been well-taught by Reynell Huyshe who impressed on his young protégé the nobility of precious metals – a factor Styles never forgot as he produced memorable trophy after trophy for clients who wanted the best and always got it. Styles was fortunate in one respect. He operated in an influential position in the 60s and 70s – a major period in the age of design. It was at a time when all that was best in a traditional sense was blended with the most forward-thinking design work. Although much of his design work was in the sporting field, his commissions included new decorations and regalia for the Armed Forces in Ghana, the four maces for Nigerian Universities and another for the Legislative Assembly of the Northern Territories of Australia. Among his other well-known and highly admired sporting trophies are those he designed for the Prudential Cup in cricket, the Rothman's Snooker Trophy and the Dunhill British Masters but the one probably admired by most people was the one he did for the Panasonic European Open. It is sterling silver gilt and like the people who proudly hold it up each year, it is a winner.

Walton Heath

Mitchell Platts of *The Times*

Peter Dazeley

When the first ball was struck in the very first European Open, Swedish sports star Sven Tumba's dream had come true. Yet the finish of the event, four days later, was almost a nightmare as bad light threatened to turn the play-off into something of a shambles. In fact a nasty situation was only avoided when the eventual winner, the American Bobby Wadkins, hit a 3-iron to three feet of the first extra hole. Everyone, except Bernard Gallacher and Gil Morgan who were also involved in the overtime battle, breathed a sigh of relief. Gallacher and Morgan just sighed, regretting their lost title chance. They were beaten by a great shot, however, and that in a way, was to characterise the championships that followed. Each year now the European Open is packed with great shots. Eleven years ago Mitchell Platts of *The Times* (then operating as a freelance) described the inaugural event this way:

Even in the big money world of golf it is rare for a player to stand on the 72nd tee in Europe needing a birdie three to win £18,000. But that was the case at Walton Heath when Scotland's Bernard Gallacher came to the 397-yard 18th on the final day of the inaugural European Open. The 30-year-old Bathgate-born Ryder Cup star, resident professional at Surrey's majestic Wentworth club, had edged towards the biggest win of his career. And ironically the programme notes on the 18th hole stated: "A splendid finishing hole. If a three is needed to win, the title is there for the taking, but - as it should be - not without the risk".

Gallacher, cocooned in concentration, knew exactly what was needed. He had been in this situation four years earlier. He recalled: "It came in the 1974 Dunlop Masters at St Pierre near Chepstow. The 18th is a short hole but it is one of the toughest in the country. I took out my 3-wood and struck a shot which gave me a tie with Gary Player. Then I took the title in the play-off. At that time it was the biggest win of my career - and that shot was the most memorable."

But at Walton Heath, Gallacher produced a shot at that last hole which ranks as one of his most forgettable. The television cameras, which had shut up exactly on time, had been instructed to start whirling again to capture those dramatic last moments. Gallacher stood on

Malcolm Gregson acknowledged the cheers when this putt dropped, but in the end his title hopes died on the greens in the inaugural Championship. He missed too many chances and finished tied fourth.

the tee. He started his backswing. But for some reason his head ducked, his shoulders came across and the ball shot out to the right. It ruined the Scot's hopes of a glorious birdie and victory - but it heightened the drama for the crowd packed around the 18th as the first European Open reached its climax.

Now Gallacher needed to provide an instant lesson in the powers of recovery in a golf tournament. It was a rabbit-like drive but he now had to compose himself because in order to tie with Americans Bobby Wadkins and Gil Morgan he had to make a four. Gallacher decided there was no point gambling with fate and going for the green. That could lead to a five, six, seven. . . history. So he collected his thoughts, pulled a five iron from his bag and hit his second short of the cross bunker that guards the front of the green. Then he wedged to 8 feet - the kind of length you could do without at that stage. No matter - he coolly holed the putt to get into the play-off.

The record books will show that Bobby Wadkins won that play-off. . . with a birdie three to the four of Gallacher and the five of Morgan. But there can be little doubt that it was Gallacher who provided the perfect climax to a first European Open packed with incident from the moment Spanish superstar Seve Ballesteros 'lost' his clubs. Seve started the event with a set of clubs borrowed from Ken Macpherson, the Walton Heath professional, and he was convinced his clubs had been stolen. In fact, through a misunderstanding, the clubs had been put into a locker in the Walton Heath clubhouse and were discovered too late. Seve shot 75 and 78 and missed the cut.

Throughout the 1978 season the rivalry on the course between Ballesteros and Nick Faldo had grown but now Faldo sensed he had a tremendous chance to bow out with a big win. In spite of a last hole disturbance on the first day when moving cameramen ruined his concentration, Faldo composed a fine 68 to lead the field. A second round 70 kept the young British player one shot clear and there was every reason to believe that Faldo would now add to the Colgate PGA title he had won earlier in the year.

Phil Sheldon

American Bobby Wadkins is congratulated by Gil Morgan after holing the winning putt in the title play-off. Bernard Gallacher, the other man beaten at the first extra hole, has little to smile about. He let his chance go at the last in the final round.

First European Open

At the moment, Faldo's closest rival was American ace Tom Weiskopf but on the third round day these two tall swingers were both "laid low". Faldo's hopes of victory were savagely scuppered when he drove out of bounds at the 513-yard 2nd and ran up an eight. It led to an incredible round that included a selection of eagles, birdies and bogeys... and finally a hole-in-one at the 191-yard 17th, caught dramatically for posterity by the quick-thinking ITV cameraman working behind the green.

Meanwhile, Weiskopf was reduced to a no-hoper when he damaged his wrist at the 11th and finished with an 81. It left the door open for blond Australian Greg Norman to accelerate smoothly into a two-shot lead... but on the last day he was to stumble to a 74 and lose his chance.

Even so, Norman still finished only one shot away from being involved in the sudden-death finish as the European Open provided an action-packed last day. Scotland's Brian Barnes and American Ed Sneed, who had sadly blown the US Masters earlier in the year, shot 68s to set the target on 286. Then another American, Jerry McGee, scored a second successive 69 to be in the clubhouse on 285.

Mac McLendon, another star from the States, put together his fourth successive 71 to finish on 284 with Norman, Faldo (71) and Malcolm Gregson (72). But Bobby Wadkins, younger brother of Lanny, had come racing through the field with the help of a devastating outward 33. The Wadkins threat seemed to be fading when he dropped shots at the 10th and 12th but the 27 year old produced a brilliant recovery. He eagled the 517-yard 14th and then birdied the 16th and 17th to complete a five-under par round and set the target on 283.

It was true that Faldo, Gregson, Norman and McLendon all had chances of making the play-off but one by one they failed to get birdies at the last hole. Morgan, second on the United States money list with almost £150,000 the previous season, joined Wadkins at the top with a 69 - helped by a 15-foot last hole birdie.

Then along came Gallacher to give the first European Open a taste of real drama and imprint the tournament on everybody's mind. But the glory went to Wadkins when he struck his three-iron approach at the first extra hole - the par 4 16th on the composite course - to 3 feet, holed the putt and took the title to land a double for the Wadkins brothers as Lanny claimed the Garden State PGA tournament in Australia the same weekend.

So there was a memorable finish to the first of the Championships that would very soon reach new heights and become firmly established for their quality of field and polished promotion. Maybe Bobby Wadkins was a little-known winner but he had played the famous course well and deserved the title of European Champion - a title everyone knew was going to grow in prestige. Sven Tumba, the man whose enthusiasm had made it all happen, was delighted. He knew he was on to a winner. What he could not have foreseen were the financial difficulties that were to arise later.

That autumn night at Walton Heath there was only euphoria.

Nick Faldo picks the ball out of the hole after making an ace at the 191 yards 17th but his title hopes had been dented with an eight at the second in the same round on Saturday.

Peter Dazeley

An untypically crooked drive into the rough at the 72nd hole left Bernard Gallacher glum. He made the play-off but lost the title.

Wadkins

Renton Laidlaw of *The Evening Standard*

Phil Sheldon

It is tough being the younger brother of a US Tour major title winner, but Bobby Wadkins, the man who won the very first European Open in 1978, has lived with it for twelve years! His brother Lanny, shorter, lighter and probably more determined, has won twelve times on the US Tour and earned over $2,000.000. He is a former US PGA Champion and lost the same event in a play-off in 1987 but Bobby, who has been on tour since 1974, has won nothing. It is one of the biggest mysteries on the bustling American circuit. Make no mistake, big Bobby – a strapping "six footer" with the physique to go with it – is no slouch. He is in many respects just a little unlucky.

In 1985 he thought he had the Sea Pines Heritage Classic in his pocket when along came another European Open winner, Bernhard Langer, to disappoint him. Just when it seemed as if the younger Wadkins brother was poised to make the breakthrough it all went wrong. He tied Langer over 72 holes all right, but lost the play-off at the first extra hole. In America no one cares who comes second!

Wadkins felt then just the way he did in Philadelphia the year after he won the European crown. This time the golfer who snatched victory from him was a former US Open champion Lou Graham. Lou, a stylish player, was six strokes off the lead in the Philadelphia IVB Classic but shot a dramatic seven under par 64 to catch Wadkins and went on to score a winning birdie at the first extra hole.

Yet the European Open success in the semi-darkness at Walton Heath in 1978 seemed to herald a rising new star bound, before long, to gain Ryder Cup honours. Sadly, the former Virginia State amateur champion has not achieved the goal of playing on the team with his brother. Bobby, who is twenty months younger than Lanny, was, like his brother, successful in junior golf in their home town of Richmond, Virginia.

Today the brothers, following in a long line of similar family double acts such as Jay and Lionel Hebert, Tom and Paul Purtzer, Jay and Jerry Haas in the States and Bernard

No one had heard much about Virginian Bobby Wadkins when he turned up at the first European Open. He was Lanny's brother – but at Walton Heath proved he was just as good a winner. Not to be outdone, Lanny won the same weekend, too, on the other side of the world.

First European Open

and Geoff Hunt in this country, often practise together on the Tour and almost every time Bobby needs help he seeks out his brother – well most of the time at any rate. To be fair, what helped Bobby most of all – as it has so many other players – was his decision to seek help in 1984 from sports psychologist Dr Bob Rotella .

What Rotella did for him was put some order into his game. "He had me develop a routine for every shot I played. I had to stick to it and it made quite a difference." says Wadkins who topped $100,000 that year.

With the mental side in good order, Wadkins now turned for additional help on his swing. When Lanny's game had gone off as it does from time to time – no matter how good a player you are, it does – he had headed for the practice range and a session or two with coach Peter Kostis. Bobby followed suit and the impact has been enormous. He has improved his average by a stroke and a half! In the last two seasons he has made not far short of $500,000. This year there have been five first-time winners on Tour, yet that first victory still eludes Bobby Wadkins who still rates as 17th best all-rounder in the weekly statistics. He is among the top ten birdie-makers but he drops too many shots at crucial points and hits too few good shots under pressure like the classic 3-iron he hit to win the European Open that weekend in September 1978 when the Wadkins family had a double celebration.

No sooner was Bobby on the telephone to tell the folks at home that he had won one of the most prestigious titles in Europe than his brother phoned from Australia confirming he had won a first prize that weekend too! The big problem Bobby has had throughout his career has been putting. He has never been comfortable on the greens throughout the fourteen years since earning his card, although his recent form would indicate that his confidence has not been dented.

"I am a slow learner," says the 37-year-old Virginian. "Perhaps it is better to say a late developer."

He is leaving it late, however, to score that important first win in the United States. Mind you, winner or not, he has earned almost 1.5 million dollars which proves you do not need to be a "killer" on the links to make a tidy living. It would be highly satisfying for him, however, if he did win on his home circuit. Meanwhile he can covet the multi-national gold-plated replica of one of the most handsome trophies in golf – the one specially designed at Garrards, the Crown jewellers, for the European Open. The fact is he won that first European Open with a master stroke that broke the hearts that week of Bernard Gallacher and Dr Gil Morgan, a Ryder Cup player from the US Tour. He can win and win well. It is a mystery why he has not done so over and over again in the years since . . . but then golf sometimes defies understanding. Maybe if he gets his putting sorted out . . . maybe it will all come right for him sometime in America!

October 19-22, 1978
Walton Heath, Tadworth, Surrey.

Prize money, £105,000
Par out: 36, Par in: 37, Yardage: 7,130

								£
1	Bobby Wadkins	USA	71	72	72	68	283	18,000.00
2	Bernard Gallacher	GB	71	71	71	70	283	8,437.00
	Gil Morgan	USA	70	73	71	69	283	8,437.50
4	Mac McLendon	USA	71	71	71	71	284	3,543.75
	Nick Faldo	GB	68	70	75	71	284	3,543.75
	Malcolm Gregson	GB	72	70	70	72	284	3,543.75
	Greg Norman	Aus.	69	72	69	74	284	3,543.75
8	Jerry McGee	USA	72	75	69	69	285	2,250.00
9	Brian Barnes	GB	72	73	73	68	286	1,821.66
	Ed Sneed	USA	71	75	72	68	286	1,821.66
	Neil Coles	GB	70	73	72	71	286	1,821.66
12	Guy Hunt	GB	73	73	72	69	287	1,411.66
	Manuel Ballesteros	Spa.	72	73	69	73	287	1,411.66
	David Graham	Aus.	72	70	70	75	287	1,411.66
15	Al. Geiberger	USA	73	73	71	71	288	1,228.00
	John Mahaffey	USA	72	74	71	71	288	1,228.00
	Tommy Horton	GB	70	73	73	72	288	1,228.00
	Ken Brown	GB	71	71	72	74	288	1,228.00
	Sam Torrance	GB	75	70	70	73	288	1,228.00
20	Mark James	GB	74	71	71	73	289	1,125.00
	Bernhard Langer	Ger.	75	74	67	73	289	1,125.00
	David Ingram	GB	75	67	72	75	289	1,125.00

Play-off: Wadkins 3, Gallacher 4, Morgan 5.

Gordon Richardson of *Golf Illustrated*

Scotland's Sandy Lyle had not won "at home" until he took the European Open title at Turnberry and won more that week than Severiano Ballesteros had in the Open two months earlier. Promoter Sven Tumba joined in the lap of honour!

Will Paton

Sven Tumba took the second European Open from leafy Surrey and the heathland of Walton Heath to the exposed links of Turnberry on the west coast of Scotland. Two years earlier the course had been the scene of a remarkable shoot-out between Jack Nicklaus and Tom Watson for the British Open title which the latter won by a shot with closing rounds of 65, 65. That was in the height of the summer, but there was some low scoring, too, in the European Championship staged in the autumn of 1979 and notably from a golfer who was on the threshold of a great career - Sandy Lyle.

As Gordon Richardson recalls in his report for *Golf Illustrated*, Lyle had been in good form throughout that summer:

Sandy Lyle's European Open win - his fourth triumph in just 99 days - was not so much a

victory as a rout. And it couldn't have come at a more opportune moment - five days before the Ryder Cup matches in America.

It was a case of "Who's going to be second?" after the husky 21 year old scored six birdies en route to an outward 30 and a spectacular closing 65. It swept him five under par on 275 - seven strokes clear of nearest challengers Dale Hayes (68) and Peter Townsend (72), earning him £17,500 and rocketing him to the top of the European money list. His £38,440 winnings total - almost all of it earned with a putter he invested £15 in at St Andrews earlier in the season - edged him over £2,000 clear of Open Champion Seve Ballesteros, who abandoned plans to miss both the TPD Championship and Dunlop Masters in the hope of matching Peter Oosterhuis's feat of topping the table in four straight seasons.

Second European Open

Declared a delighted Lyle: "I suppose my Dad will want a Rolls Royce for Christmas now." Lyle's magical victory sent the spirits of Europe's Ryder Cup men soaring sky-high as they headed for Heathrow and a confrontation with the Americans which they lost.

Starting out a stroke behind overnight leaders Neil Coles and Mark James, Lyle, winner of the British Airways/Avis, Scandinavian and Scottish Professionals titles since the start of June, spread-eagled the field with that sensational opening sprint - 343, 232, 4 against a par of 444, 343, 5.

He explained: "I holed a 10-footer at the first and a 10-yarder at the third but after a two at the fourth I was sure I was going to drop at least one when I drove in the rough at the next and could only hack the ball 40 yards forward. But from 60 yards out I knocked it straight into the cup, holed from 18 feet at the next, then came out of a bunker to 18 inches at the 7th - I thought I was dreaming.'

It was all over bar the shouting, with Neil Coles slipping to a 74 to share 4th place on 283 with Tommy Horton, bouncing back to form with a 66. James, out in 40, took eleven strokes more than his brilliant third round with a 75 for joint 6th spot on 284 which tied him with Ballesteros who birdied three of the last six holes for a 71, and Sam Torrance who closed with 70.

Hayes, who had three birdies in four holes from the 14th, and Townsend, brilliantly maintaining his Canadian PGA Championship form after a putting lesson from Doug Sanders, won £9,025 each for joint second. Horton and Coles collected £4,227 apiece and Ballesteros, James and Torrance £2,233, which left the top four in the money list looking like this: Lyle £38,440, Ballesteros £36,335, James £31,200 and Hayes £29,886.

Lyle, who finished with a flourish by birdieing 17 and 18 after dropping strokes at 15 and 16, explained: "My target this year was simply to make the Ryder Cup side and let the rest take care of itself - I guess I just got lucky. I spent three to four hours a day practising my short game during the Irish Open on Joe Carr's course at Sutton and my Dad has kept an eye on my swing."

Peter Dazeley

A closing round of 74 meant that Neil Coles did not win as much as he would have liked, but he refused to blame the elbow injury that had bothered him at Lytham earlier in the season.

Lyle, who had put weight back on after his mid-season bout of glandular fever was now assured a place in the Lancôme line-up in Paris, and was set for an invitation to the Suntory World Match Play Championship as well. He knew that if he stayed top of the table he would be able to demand anything up to £75,000 in appearance fees in 1980, which he planned to launch by playing in three or four US tournaments.

The further good news was that he would definitely be defending his European Open title. Organiser Sven Tumba confirmed the event would go on in 1980 in the London area.

Two men, James and Coles, dominated the third day that year at Turnberry - James shooting 64 and Coles 66 to share the lead after overnight rain flooded greens and delayed the start. James, starting seven behind leaders Ballesteros, Lyle and Ken Brown, gave notice of intent to challenge American Mark Hayes' course record 63, set in the 1977 Open, by opening with two birdies. He was out in 30 and it would have been 29 but for a careless four at the short 6th. It would not have been James's first sub-30 nine. He was home in 29 during the Welsh Classic and he had showed with a finishing 65 to win the Carroll's Irish Open at Portmarnock that tough championship links held no terrors for him. In the end a fluffed 4 at the last cost him a share of that record. He had only 25 putts - twelve fewer than in the second round.

Coles, revealing the elbow injury which forced him to retire during the Open, had cleared up, confessed he'd "got out of jail" by sinking a 12-yard chip and a 7-yard putt early on. But Neil, seeking his first win since the 1977 TPD Championship, showed no apparent ill-effects from the hernia, which forced him to rule himself out of the Ryder Cup and opt for an operation in the November, as he sped home in 32. Howard Clark underlined his return to form with a pair of eagles in a 67 which lifted him within three strokes of James and Coles. Lyle stayed in touch with a 72 for 210 but Brown ran up a six at the last after driving into a bush for a 74 and 212 and Ballesteros slumped to a 75 for 213 - four behind.

Declared Seve: "My cold is much worse. I didn't sleep at all last night. I feel weak and I can't see properly."

So it was James and Coles, from Lyle and Townsend, with Clark, Brown and Jose Canizares two further back, a stroke clear of Ballesteros and Garry Cullen. At the start of the week attention had focused on star imports Bobby Wadkins, the defending Champion, Larry Nelson, lying second to Tom Watson with £125,000 in the US money list, US PGA Champion David Graham, of Australia and Doug Sanders. On the first day Graham, heading for his best US season with nearly £90,000 prize money, was the best of them with a wind-defying 73. Wadkins took 75, Nelson and Sanders 77. Sanders then opted out, a victim of tennis elbow, but a last round 68 gave Nelson a share of 15th place on 289. Wadkins had the same score, but Graham chalked up 297 - only four behind a surprisingly out-of-touch Tony Jacklin.

Surprise first-round leader by a stroke from Ballesteros and South African Vinny Baker was Britain's Tony Charnley on 68. Ballesteros highlighted his first round by holing a 20-yard bunker shot for a two.

A stroke behind were Canizares, Cullen, Brown and Bob Charles, with Lyle on 71. Lyle, Brown and Ballesteros leaped to the front on 138 after a second round which saw two more retirements - Brian Huggett for family reasons and New Zealand's Simon Owen, who jarred his back in practice.

Ballesteros, now thoroughly miserable with the onset of that cold, came home in 33 for a repeat 69, while Lyle stirred hopes of an action replay of his duel with Seve in Sweden by snapping up four birdies in seven holes round the turn for a 67 in which he had only 26 putts. Brown, relishing the less windy conditions which favoured his fade, snapped up five birdies in his 68 but admitted he was lucky to get away with a five at the 10th after hitting his drive only 40 yards.

They led by two from Charles, Canizares and Townsend, with Yorkshire's Gordon Brand needing only 25 putts in a 66 for 141 after a putting lesson from his wife, proette Lyn Ghent, on their hotel carpet. But in the end nothing would stop Lyle's roller-coaster victory.

The big prize went to Lyle but just as important, in its own way, was the £500 Tony Charnley, the first round leader picked up! For long enough he had played in the shadow of Ken Brown at Harpenden Common. Ken lived on the

Seve has never won the European Open. A heavy cold left him weak at Turnberry, but he still finished joint sixth with the help of three late birdies on the final day.

Tony Duffy

Second European Open

Larry Nelson may have won three of golf's so-called "majors" but back in 1979 he was unknown when he flew in to Turnberry. By the end of the week everyone knew him and respected his talent. He loved playing links golf for the first time.

David Cannon

course, Tony at Luton. Ken turned pro and a year later Tony, an England Youth international and Carris Trophy winner, followed suit.

On the tournament circuit, Brown had had the success and gained all the attention – until the first round of the European Open, when Charnley shocked the international field by taking a one-stroke lead with a two under par 68. And it all came about because he decided to miss the Swiss Open and called in on the pro at Harpenden Common, Nigel Lawrence. While there he picked up a putter belonging to Lawrence, a centre-shafted Craigton, tried it out, and did a deal with Lawrence, buying it for £4. And what a bargain it proved to be! He had twelve single putts – eight of them to save par – and took 26 putts in all as he battled his way round the windy Ailsa course.

Charnley's tournament career had nearly come to a sad end a few weeks earlier – he was being pressed by his bank, as he was overdrawn, and after talking things over with his father, had made up his mind to quit golf and take any sort of job to pay off his debts.

Then his luck changed. The captain of Harpenden Common club, Ray Smith, made him a gift of £500 to keep him on the circuit, and although his highest finish had been 23rd in the Welsh Classic he picked up £320 there and £360 at the English Classic and altogether his cheques had added up to £1,800 before the European Open.

"I've settled my debts at the bank, have a few hundred pounds left and hope my luck holds out," said 24 year-old Charnley. "Certainly, the putter made the difference - the strange thing is that Nigel Lawrence is a left-hander, but apparently the right-handed touch is the magic one."

Charnley's final placing at Turnberry earned him £500.

Although Lyle grabbed all the headlines at Turnberry, there were glowing reports, too, of the slightly built American Larry Nelson who arrived unknown despite being second on the US money list at the time to Tom Watson.

Watson, of course was way out at the top of the list with an incredible $440,000 in prize-money after another super season which had brought him five victories for the second year in a row. But Nelson - who celebrated his 32nd birthday on the Monday after the European Open - had been quietly pocketing big cheques, which added up to almost $250,000.

He had been on the US Tour since 1974 and picked up his first tournament victory in 1979 when he won the Inveraray Classic. Then in consecutive weeks, he tied for the Memphis Classic, losing the play-off to Gil Morgan, won the Western Open and tied for fourth place in the US Open. Yet Nelson might never have taken to golf had it not been for his wife Gayle. Nelson was keen on baseball and basketball, but hurt his right arm pitching at baseball and as he could play the game no longer, he looked for something else to do. That was in 1969, when he was 21.

"My wife bought me a set of clubs for Christmas and I decided I would start playing - I had never played golf before," Nelson said at Turnberry. "I think it was meant as a hint - just to get me out of the house - I guess!"

He took the clubs, a Doug Sanders set, to a driving range and found he had a flair for the game - and fourteen months later, broke 70. "I took an assistant's job in Bert Seagrave's shop at Pine Tree in Kennesaw, Georgia, where I live, and he helped me with my game - even now, I go back to him when I have problems," said Nelson. And Nelson, who turned pro nine months after taking up the game, moved on to the mini-tour and then finished runner-up in the Florida State Open, his only 72-hole tournament before winning his US player's card in 1973. For some time on the Tour, Nelson said he was not sure he could compete with the established stars. "I decided I was either going to learn how to compete with the top guys or quit," he said.

And, like so many of the relative newcomers to the American circuit, he had little interest in either the Ryder Cup or the British Open.

"Our main concern, of course, is getting into the top 60 - and staying there," Nelson told reporter Alan Booth, as he admired the panoramic view of the Ailsa and Arran courses from the Turnberry Hotel. "But by winning two tournaments, I found myself in the Ryder Cup list and all of a sudden, all the guys were talking about the match and before I knew where I was, I was as keen as any of them to take part.

Nelson did not find Turnberry easy - buffeted by the wind on the first day he came in with 77 and followed with 70 and 74, but a last-day 68 was some consolation as he finished on 289 - nine over par. "These courses need some taming," he said. "That ninth hole, by the lighthouse, where it blows pretty hard, gave me nightmares. I took five the first day, then six and followed with seven. But I got its measure on the last day, getting my par 4."

Nelson, slightly balding, standing 5 feet 9 inches and weighing 11 stone showed his courage against the conditions and with his amiable nature and friendly outlook on life could become a top star, reported Alan Booth in 1979. Nelson has since won a US Open and two US PGA titles.

Will Paton

England's Howard Clark (with long hair) and Jose-Maria Canizares of Spain look on at the 17th as Sandy Lyle of Scotland continues his demolition job on the Ailsa course on the final day.

Lyle

David Davies of *The Guardian*

Don Morley

Sandy Lyle is, on his playing record, the best golfer ever produced in the British Isles. That is not to say he is the most charismatic, the most dominating personality or the most attractive golfer to watch, but in terms of success on the golf course, he has no equal.

That, of course, is a big statement, but then Lyle has some superb achievements to justify making it. He has not, of course, won as many of what we now call major championships as some of the Toms, James and Harrys of the past and there is an argument as old as the Morris's, the Braids and the Vardons when it comes to comparisons between past players and the modern stars.

But just as I believe that Jack Nicklaus is the greatest golfer of them all, and just as I accept that Bobby Jones and Ben Hogan *may* have been as great, given modern equipment and conditions , so I also take leave to believe that the sports practitioners of today are vastly more skilled than their predecessors. As Severiano Ballesteros said, only four hours after his victory at Royal Lytham and St Anne's, Nicklaus's record is out of reach of the players of today, because standards have risen so dramatically since the American compiled the early part of it in the 60s. Ballesteros pointed out that every measurable sport had improved enormously, so why not golf?

It would be astonishing if golf had not improved pro rata with other sports, and it would be astonishing, in my view, if it did not go on doing so. Equipment will not improve, or more probably will not be allowed to improve much further, but the scope for human improvement, not least on the mental side, is still immense. Which is where we come back to Sandy Lyle.

He is Britain's first truly successful production-line golfer. Lyle hit his first golf ball –it went 80 yards! – at the age of three and a half and from that moment he was literally never off the golf course. As the son of Alex Lyle, the professional at Hawkestone Park in Shropshire, he had access to everything a budding professional could

Sandy Lyle's European Open victory heralded the start of a sparkling professional career that has given him world acclaim and record earnings. He is the first man to win $1,000,000 in American prize-money and £1,000,000 in European!

need and in addition, as that first shot indicated, he had the eye and the co-ordination that comes as a gift – it cannot be learned.

He was, of course, allowed his childhood, running free around the beautiful countryside in which Hawkstone is located, but there was always golf in the background. Barely a day would go by without shots being hit, and soon enough, when Lyle reached his early teens, his father instituted a programme which was designed to make him into a golfer. Nobody knew then how good he was to become, of course, but Alex realised there was a raw talent and was determined to make the most of it. Talent he could mould; technique he could impart; temperament – well, they would just have to wait and see.

When he first began to compete, Lyle did so as a boy with a man's frame. At the age of fourteen he took size 11 shoes, but his father was careful not to ask too much. He gave his boy a slow swing, one that would not overtax him and would allow him to learn the finer points fully as he went along. As Lyle got stronger the speed of the swing was gradually increased and as he moved into his late teens he took up some rudimentary physical exercise, using a static bicycle or running through the Shropshire lanes. It was, of its kind, a carefully planned programme, possible in this country only for a golf professional and his son. And yet if you were to repeat it to the average East German athlete and represent it for what it is in golf – advanced training – he would surely laugh in your face.

But Lyle succeeded at every level. He won every Midland title worth having. Although Scottish he was resident in England and played for England at Boys, Youths and Senior level in the same year, 1975. He only delayed turning professional immediately because the Family Lyle, by now sensing something extraordinary in him, wanted, in the words of the Frank Sinatra song, to make all the stops along the way. That meant adding selection for the Walker Cup team to his record and that was duly done in 1977.

His amateur education was now complete.

So was his physical moulding and the essentials of his golf game. He was by now 6 feet 1 inch, 13 stone 5lbs and blessed with the long back and comparatively short legs that seem to suit the best golfers. He could hit the ball further than almost anybody in the country, had a glorious touch around the greens and while, at times, he could not putt any better than Auntie Mabel, at other times everything would go in.

The next step was professional golf and while father Alex had by now no qualms about talent or technique, the game is full of

Sandy, who had his first club at the age of three, had an impressive junior and amateur career before turning professional - a logical step for the son of a pro.

Birmingham Post & Mail

23

Second European Open

Golf Photography International

It may be a heavy trophy but golfers do not come much stronger than Sandy Lyle who thrilled all his Scottish fans with his impressive success.

players who have had both and still not made it in the harsher world where every shot means either more, or less, money at the end of the week. Within two years Lyle had topped the Order of Merit and was a Ryder Cup player.

He was also one of the first European Open champions, a win which confirmed in his mind his ability to play at that level. It also confirmed his arrival with certain bookmakers who, at the start of the week, had him at 33-1 for the Championship. The Press tent availed itself of ludicrous odds like that and after the next four days Lyle was never to be found at those odds again.

Lyle was one behind Mark James and Neil Coles at the start of the final round. One hour and a half later Lyle's challengers were almost literally out of sight, as he started with six birdies in seven holes. The fifth hole sticks in my mind. A poor, drawn drive; a second hacked further up the thick rough on the left and, with a pin on the left side of the green of a hole that dog-legs left, the question was whether Lyle would take six or seven. He hit a sand wedge straight into the hole. For those who recall Turnberry, the site of that Championship, Lyle started: (1) Drive, wedge, 15-feet putt. (2) Drive, seven iron, two putts. (3) Drive, six iron, 30-feet putt. (4) Seven iron, 5-feet putt. (5) Drive, nine iron, sand wedge. (6) Three iron, 21-feet putt. (7) Drive, three wood, sand wedge, 9-inch putt. Golf like that seemed to answer the question of survival on the Tour, except, of course, that expectations had by now become considerably greater. Lyle, who now represented his native land of Scotland – his parents are both Scottish even if he was born in England – had to win a major in order to satisfy not only the people who demanded it of him but also to fulfil his own talent. For the next four years he was never out of the top five in the money list, winning "ordinary" tournaments with seeming nonchalance, earning the nickname of either 'Sleepy' Sandy, for obvious reasons, or 'Sunday' Sandy because so much of his money came from charging 66s in the last round.

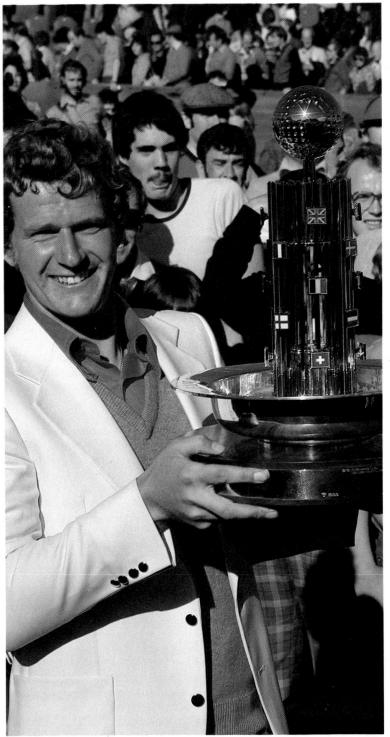

Then at the end of 1984, in the unlikely, but luxurious, surroundings of Kapalua on the Hawaiian resort island of Mauii, there occurred a significant shift in the emphasis of Lyle's career. He had gone to the event, the Kapalua International, with no more than a vague intention of making some money and having a holiday. The field turned out to be a good one, however, with most of the leading American tour players there and Lyle realised that even to make a decent cheque he would have to play quite well. Rather to his surprise, at the end of a very long season, he began to play not just quite well, but very well. In fact, in difficult windy conditions, he won in a canter.

Almost without him knowing it, the last important ingredient had been added to his golfing make-up. he now had the knowledge, the certainty, that he could beat the best Americans in their own conditions. Even if *we* had suspected it, *he* had always known he had the temperament: what *he* was unsure of was whether the others were simply better players. Now he knew they were not.

And so we come to the years of Lyle's pomp. Within eight months of Kapalua he had won the Open Championship at Royal St George's, the first Briton to do so since Tony Jacklin had won at Lytham in 1969; in 1986 he won the Greater Greensboro Open; in 1987 he took the title that the US Tour holds most dear, the Tournament Players' Championship (now simply called The Players' Championship) at the Tour headquarters at Sawgrass near Jacksonville in Florida. This year, of course, he has won the Phoenix Open, the Greater Greensboro Open again, and one of the most unforgettable US Masters that, I suspect there will ever be. All that is mixed in with regular European tour victories, including, this year, the Dunhill Masters, and he has made more money, on the course, on both sides of the Atlantic, than any other Briton – £1,000,000 in Britain, $1,000,000 in the States. Unbelievably, he went to the top of the US money list in the middle of April, staying there for over three months, as the

remainder of that talented but hugely overpaid Tour tried and failed to overtake him. He also forged a place for himself in history, for not only was he the first Briton to win the US Masters, he did so in indelible fashion. To birdie the last hole to win, to do it after driving into a fairway bunker, after hitting a 7-iron out of that bunker on to the green and having a ball roll back down the slope 15 feet towards the hole, and then holing from 10 feet for the win: all of that was sporting drama of the most intense and exhilarating kind.

It also denoted the fulfilment of one of the great talents in our golfing history, a talent that seems certain to express itself still further, for Lyle, at 30, has time to amass a record that will withstand the closest scrutiny. He is, in my view, our best so far. It may not stay that way, as golf grows and adopts more sophisticated training techniques, but for the present he and his immense talent are there for all to enjoy.

September 6-9, 1979
Ailsa Course, Turnberry Hotel, Ayrshire.

Prize money; £105,000
Par out: 35, Par in: 35, Yardage: 6,875

								£
1	Sandy Lyle	GB	71	67	72	65	275	17,500.00
2	Dale Hayes	SA	72	72	70	68	282	9,025.00
	Peter Townsend	GB	72	68	70	72	282	9,025.00
4	Tommy Horton	GB	74	72	71	66	283	4,227.50
	Neil Coles	GB	73	70	66	74	283	4,227.50
6	Sam Torrance	GB	71	72	71	70	284	2,233.33
	Severiano Ballesteros	Spa.	69	69	75	71	284	2,233.33
	Mark James	GB	73	72	64	75	284	2,233.33
9	Howard Clark	GB	74	71	67	73	285	1,675.00
	Jose-Maria Canizares	Spa.	70	70	72	73	285	1,675.00
11	Ken Brown	GB	70	68	74	75	287	1,500.00
12	Bill Longmuir	GB	73	73	72	79	288	1,400.00
	Des Smyth	Ire.	73	68	76	71	288	1,400.00
	Gordon Brand	GB	75	66	74	73	288	1,400.00
15	Larry Nelson	USA	77	70	74	68	289	1,143.00
	Noel Ratcliffe	Aus.	75	68	77	69	289	1,143.75
	Robin Fyfe	GB	75	70	75	69	289	1,143.75
	Robbie Stewart	SA	77	70	72	70	289	1,143.75
	Bobby Wadkins	USA	75	71	71	72	289	1,143.75
	Brian Waites	GB	72	72	73	72	289	1,143.75
	John Morgan	GB	75	70	70	74	289	1,143.75
	Manuel Pinero	Spa.	74	72	70	73	289	1,143.75

1980
Walton Heath

Gordon Richardson of *Golf Illustrated*

No one knew it at the time but there was a prophetic look about the final leader-board in the third European Open back at Walton Heath. An American won the title again. This time it was Tom Kite who took the honours and predicted that while the Europeans had to win the Ryder Cup at some stage it would not be in 1981 at the Surrey course. He was absolutely correct, although, in fairness to a European side which was growing in strength, the Americans brought over their strongest team in years with Jack Nicklaus and Lee Trevino in the vanguard of their challenge. We lost 18½ - 9½ but the revolution was just around the corner and the European Open was providing top-level competition to fully test our players.

Once again Gordon Richardson was on the spot to record the most precious moments from another fine championship. This report originally appeared in *Golf Illustrated*:

Twice the European Open has been played at Walton Heath. Twice the winner has been an American who was not among the top twenty on the US Tour - Bobby Wadkins in 1978 and Tom Kite in 1980. With Lon Hinkle and Leonard Thompson (also currently out of the American top twenty) occupying joint second place this time, it augurs badly for Britain and Europe's Ryder Cup chances over the same course next summer. For although Kite (75) and Hinkle (77) finished tamely no one emerged from the pack to mount a serious challenge, Sandy Lyle, third overnight, crashing to a sad 79 after an incredible 44 to the turn.

Kite's first big win for almost two years came as a weak climax to the contest which never quite caught fire. Despite three putts at the last he finished eight under par on 284 -one ahead of Thompson (71) and Hinkle, who three-putted both the 16th and 18th to earn £17,500, his countrymen collecting £9,025 each. Dale Hayes of South Africa, who cracked his driver in round two and switched effectively to one from a barrel-load of 600 he bought for a dollar a club from a New York dealer to stock his Pretoria shop, nipped into fourth place by chipping in to birdie the last for a 71,286 and £5,000.

Bernard Gallacher, beaten in a play-off by Wadkins two years earlier, holed a monster for par at the 72nd for a 74 to share fifth place on 287 with Ryder Cup teammates Des Smyth (70), Mark James (70), Sam Torrance (72) and the up-and-coming Bernhard Langer of West Germany (73), the five earning £2,381 apiece. The bespectacled Texan, Kite, was apologetic about his low-key win - he blamed a car horn for his only three-putt of the event at the last. He then talked about the up-coming Ryder Cup the following year.

"By the law of averages you must win one some time. It was much closer than the 17-11 scoreline suggests, when I played in the States last year.

"Walton Heath ought to favour your golfers. We generally play target golf on well-watered parkland courses. But you've got to remember a heck of a lot of Americans have experience of links-type golf through playing in your Open. Having the European Open here twice means plenty of our fellows have some knowledge of this course and I think we will do well here."

The last round surprise was Sandy Lyle. His form over the opening holes was in sharp

Peter Dazeley

Bernhard Langer got out of trouble well to finish joint fifth.

Peter Dazeley

contrast to when he won at Turnberry. Then he birdied six of the first seven en route to a 65. This time he dropped seven shots in the first six. The only common factor was that he chipped in both times - this time at the third for a triple bogey seven after hacking one out of bounds and twice moving his ball only inches in thick heather by the green.

He battled home in 35 for joint 15th place to gain some consolation, for although Order-of-Merit leader Greg Norman had the best-of-the-day 69 for tenth place on 288, he won only £450 more than the Scot - so the race to finish No. 1 in the European money list remained wide open, especially as Severiano Ballesteros slipped to a closing 77 to trail three behind Lyle on 294. A third-round 77, in this multi-sponsored event hosted by the Dutch petro-chemical giant DSM and the Province of Limburg, sent Denis Durnian slithering back into the pack, but the 30-year-old Bolton man was the star of the first day with a five below par 68, which left him a stroke ahead of Hinkle, Gallacher, James, Jeff Hall, Carl Mason and American Jim Colbert.

Durnian, who spent two spells countering hard times by working on the night shift in an Australian ice cream factory, began his golfing career by hitting practice balls off the decks of cargo ships while serving in the Merchant Navy. Although he tied for victory in the 1978 Greater Manchester Open, losing a play-off to Brian Barnes, slim moustachioed Denis had fallen on hard times and admitted he was contemplating quitting the full-time tournament circuit to seek a club job when in stepped the Dunhill company with the offer to sponsor him, Gary Cullen, Donald Armour and Billy McColl for three years. Durnian, who made an eagle and seven birdies, held his ground on Friday with a two below par 71 for 139, but he had to settle for third place behind Hinkle, who produced a majestic record 65 for a twelve below par 134, and Kite, who described his 67 as one of the best rounds of his career. Veteran Australian Bruce Devlin and James were on 140 and Gary Cullen on 141. Hinkle waited 30 minutes to tee off after a thunderstorm halted play. Doubtless the dramatic softening up of the course allowed the big American to play more

American Lon Hinkle powered his way up the leader board on the third day.

Third European Open

familiar target golf, and helped him accumulate seven birdies and an eagle and drop only one stroke to par.

Happy men all three, were Hinkle, Kite and Durnian, but decidedly unhappy were Peter Oosterhuis, who missed the cut by a stroke on 149 to continue an unhappy season (he was deep down in 94th place in the US money league with a bare £12,000), Nick Faldo on 150 and Tony Jacklin on 153.

The third round had looked like being a follow-my-leader affair, with Hinkle moving fourteen under par after eleven holes, but Kite was hanging on to him at eleven under. Lyle, despite pulling his drive out of bounds over the fence at the second, was making a great effort to hold on to his title, surrounding his seven,at that hole with a pair of birdie threes and making three more birdies from the sixth to turn in 33. Birdie number six at the 14th swept him eight under par, but instead of trailing seven behind he found himself only four adrift of the leader as Hinkle suddenly and unaccountably opened the door by dropping three strokes in the last six holes for a sad 74, to finish the day only one ahead of Kite.

If the last day was anticlimatic, the Championship still produced a class winner. Tom Kite, who won £17,500, was congratulated by an increasingly worried Sven Tumba for whom, sadly, it would be the last with him in charge.

In the three years of the European Open, there had been a commendable and strong international field and the transatlantic challengers in 1980 included a surprise visitor. Bruce Devlin of Australia, who had joined the growing Senior Tour, made a comeback at Walton Heath to big-time golf. The 42 year old had virtually dropped out of tournament golf after eight big victories in the mid-70s to concentrate on his golf course and condominium building and shirt-manufacturing businesses, as well as his TV commentating career.

He had played a restricted schedule but finished 9th in Greensboro and 12th in the US Open to earn himself a place in the 1981 Championship and the US Masters. His two opening 70s at Walton Heath hinted that his first big win since the 1972 US Industries

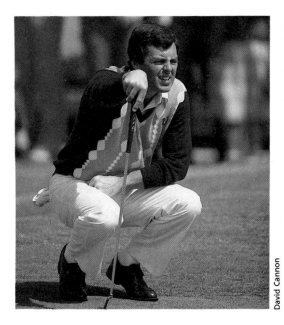

David Cannon

Bernard Gallacher, always a favourite with the crowd, was in contention right through to the last round.

Classic might not be far away.

Devlin, who seems to produce his best when the prizes are biggest - he took the £12,000 Carling World jackpot at Royal Birkdale in 1965 and the £25,000 Alcan top cheque at Portmarnock in 1970 - explained: "I lost my appetite for competition completely in the late 70s. "I became too involved with my other interests, but it's coming back. There's nothing to compare with the feeling you get when you're winning at golf."

Devlin, who is currently engaged on five US golf course projects and would like to tackle one in Britain, spoke of his concern for the future of TV golf - and tournament golf in general - in America:

"I'm convinced there has got to be a big cut-back - maybe ten or a dozen events less on the screens next year. I heard recently that 30-second advertising spots on one golf telecast were selling at $3,000 compared with the normal $28,000. The problem is there are too many tournaments and also, I must say that some of the younger players aren't doing sufficient to make them more colourful and interesting. Too many just walk out and do their thing in the Pro-Ams instead of putting something into it. It's a shame because a lot of them have plenty of talent."

28

Portrait of a Winner
Kite

David Davies of *The Guardian*

Ask the average golf fan whom he thinks might figure in the top five of the all-time, career money-winners list in America and he might well come up with the top two, Jack Nicklaus and Tom Watson. He might also essay a guess at, say, Ben Crenshaw or Fuzzy Zoeller or even Arnold Palmer.

But he might not name Tom Kite, and that would be a considerable mistake, for this marvellously modest, schoolmasterly, bespectacled man is, in fact, the third heaviest earner on the golf course in American history, with a staggering $3,700,000. Thomas O. Kite junior, 5 feet 8½ inches and weighing 13 stone, is, beyond any question, one of the great success stories in any sport. In each of the last seven years he has had at least one win on the US Tour. He has represented and captained his country internationally; he has played Walker and Ryder Cup golf and on top of all that won the 1979 Bob Jones Award, given annually to the year's most distinguished golfing sportsman. Kite is not just a very good golfer, he is one of the sport's great ambassadors and an exceedingly pleasant person too.

But for all that, he is, when he thinks about one aspect of his career, an extremely dissatisfied person as well. Tom Kite has done just about everything in golf except win a major championship and that, in what is admittedly an unfair sport, is the unkindest cut of all. Few people have tried harder over the years. Almost no top class golfer has a game more fitted for the winning of majors and, after a shaky start to his career in the matter of temperament, he has shown, repeatedly in the years of his maturity, that winning is no longer a problem. What Kite has lacked is the luck. The simple good fortune that goes with the winning of every major championship, the right break at the right time.

Two moments stand out in recent years. The Open Championship at Royal St George's in 1985 was won, of course, by Sandy Lyle – a player who has repeatedly crossed Kite's path, with varying results. But after nine holes of the final round the leader, after a marvellous outward half of 32, was

Kite. He then hit a good drive down the 10th and was faced with a relatively simple shot to the green. He admittedly played a poorish stroke, dragging the ball left, but it was then that he got the kind of break that eats into a golfer's soul. Instead of going into one of the two huge bunkers on the left, leaving him with a straightforward sand shot of the kind that professionals *expect* to get up and down, the ball trickled down between the two into an almost impossible position. A probable four or a possible five became an actual six and Kite was effectively from that moment out of the Championship.

Compare that with Lyle's experience at the 14th in the same round. He had an awful drive hooked deep into elephant grass; he hacked out; hit a two-iron 220 yards to the right edge of the green; then sank a forty-feet putt for birdie! Then the mind's eye moves forward a season, to Augusta and the 1986 US Masters. Tom Kite has a record at Augusta which makes you think every year that this must surely be the time he breaks through. Eight times in the last decade he has finished in the top six and his scoring

Studious Tom Kite whose golf has been good enough for long enough to win a major – but somehow there is always someone better on the day.

Phil Sheldon

29

record over that wonderful golf course is better than any other non-winner. The only golfers with better averages are Watson, Nicklaus and Ballesteros, who, between them, have won the championship ten times. In 1986 all of that trio were in contention, along with Bernhard Langer and Greg Norman, and, of course, the inevitable Kite. It was to be the Year of Jack Nicklaus, taking his sixth Masters at the age of 46, but, of all the people who could have at least taken the Championship into extra holes, Kite came the closest.

Standing on the 18th tee he knew that he needed a birdie to tie Nicklaus and, under that pressure, hit a superb drive. He followed that with a second which finished 10 feet right of the pin, a position which delighted him for he had practised from there prior to the tournament and knew the pace and line of the putt.

He appeared to hit it perfectly. It missed on the left. "I made that putt," he said afterwards, unable to believe the evidence of his scorecard! "The ball just did not go in. Honest to God. I made it so many times in the practice rounds, seven or eight times, and it never broke left once."

There are two problems of perception to go with the sad fact of not having won a championship. He is perceived as being a lesser golfer than, say, Andy North who has won two US Opens, or Dave Stockton who has won two US PGA Championships, or Larry Mize, or Lou Graham or a dozen other players who, in career terms, are hardly fit to be on the same tee as Kite. Then, of course, he is perceived in the media as being "the best golfer never to have won a major," which must be the most aggravating tag of all.

"The one thing missing in my life is a major," he said recently. "If I got run over by car overnight and couldn't play anymore I'd still be pleased with my career because I've done far more than most. But when they assess you at the end, it's not the money, it's the majors. And there are only a few of those in your lifetime, which in itself creates problems. You have to keep yourself from

saying 'must win a major, must win a major'. It's all too easy to put too much extra pressure on yourself. When I win on the Tour it's not because I do anything different, it's because it's my week. Last year when I won the Kemper I didn't do anything special, and I won by seven shots. Not doing anything special works. If you do something a particular way for 28 tournaments and in general it works, why do it any other way for the four Grand Slam events? For quite a few years I did not win on the US Tour, but then I did and got over the hump. I guess it's the same with majors, there is an extra level to be attained."

Kite won his European Open at Walton Heath in 1980 and, as he is still only 38, there is time yet for him to climb the major mountain triumphantly. In the meantime, he plays, and has played, some of the most marvellous golf imaginable, not a little of it at Walton Heath. He was a member of what was probably the strongest golf team ever assembled, the US Ryder Cup side of 1981. The names read like a recent history of the best of the American golf: Nicklaus, Watson, Trevino, Crenshaw, Floyd, Irwin, Nelson, Rogers, Lietzke, Pate, Miller – all at

Winner Tom Kite receives the trophy from HRH Prince Bernhard of the Netherlands with promoter Sven Tumba looking on. Months later the event was under new management.

the peak of their form. It was scarcely a contest, with the score USA 17 – Great Britain and Ireland 8, and one of the reasons for that crushing score was form like that displayed by Kite. In the final singles series against Sandy Lyle, playing at the top of his form (and when he does most people would put their mortgage on him winning), Kite was unbelievably good. After 16 holes Lyle was, in fact, eight-under-par and shaking hands – a loser! Kite was an incredible ten-under-par.

It was an experience that would have scarred many a young player, but Lyle does not think as other men do; he simply accepted that on the day he was not good enough and went on playing in his usual way. Not for him the frenzied assault on the practice ground trying to find out how to go round in ten under every day. As luck, or perhaps some astute draw-making, would have it, Kite found himself in the same half as Lyle in the following year's Suntory World Match Play Championship at Wentworth. They duly met in the semi-final and when Kite realised that that was to be the case, remarked: "I know he'll be coming at me with blood in his eyes. But I've never shied away from a fight yet and I've shown him once what I can do."

But Sandy is more the silent killer type than a blood-in-the eyes man and whether or not revenge even entered his head it certainly came his way. Lyle played superbly for the first eighteen holes and Kite was six down. All Lyle had to do now was make a solid start to the second round and he was as good as in the final.

But, infuriating golfer that he can be, he allowed Kite to win the first two holes of the afternoon and the American's hope of a recovery was clearly on the cards. Then they came to the third at Wentworth, which before they altered it this year, had a two-tier green which had become unfair because the bottom tier sloped too severely.

He had played two shots just short of the green and attempted a chip and run. His first shot, with an 8-iron, almost reached the top of the bank before stopping and running

all the way back down to his feet. Kite changed clubs, to a 7-iron, and tried again. Same thing. Then he tried again with the same club and did the same thing again.

As he stood there trying to contain his anger, a voice came from the crowd. "Take your driver, Tom," it said and to Kite's great credit he managed a smile. By now he was playing six and this time the ball definitely crested the tier, so much so that it ran off the back of the green and Kite had to chip back, dead, with a 9-iron. He had taken eight, Lyle by now had four for it from 12 feet and the hole was conceded. With it, in effect, went the match and as the two men walked to the fourth tee, both were grinning, chatting amiably.

It takes a talent for golf to do what Tom Kite has done in the sport – and it takes a talent for life to play it and survive it, despite the disappointments, as he has done.

September 4-7, 1980
Walton Heath, Golf Club, Tadworth, Surrey.

Prize money; £105,000
Par out: 36, Par in: 37, Yardage: 7,230

							£
1	Tom Kite	USA	71	67	71	75	284	17,500.00
2	Leonard Thompson	USA	72	70	72	71	285	9,025.00
	Lon Hinkle	USA	69	65	74	77	285	9,025.00
4	Dale Hayes	SA	73	73	69	71	286	5,000.00
5	Des Smyth	Ire.	72	72	73	70	287	2,381.00
	Mark James	GB	69	71	77	70	287	2,381.00
	Sam Torrance	GB	71	71	73	72	287	2,381.00
	Bernhard Langer	Ger.	71	73	70	73	287	2,381.00
	Bernard Gallacher	GB	69	73	71	74	287	2,381.00
10	Greg Norman	Aus.	72	73	74	69	288	1,600.00
11	Brian Waites	GB	73	73	71	72	289	1,500.00
12	John O'Leary	Ire.	73	72	72	73	290	1,400.00
	Howard Clark	GB	73	73	71	73	290	1,400.00
	Jim Colbert	USA	69	75	72	74	290	1,400.00
15	Denis Watson	SA	72	75	72	72	291	1,250.00
	Hugh Baiocchi	SA	74	71	72	74	291	1,250.00
	Sandy Lyle	GB	72	70	70	79	291	1,250.00
18	Neil Coles	GB	75	72	75	70	292	1,100.00
	Gary Cullen	GB	72	69	76	75	292	1,100.00
	Mark McNulty	SA	75	71	71	75	292	1,100.00
	Graham Burroghs	GB	75	72	70	75	292	1,100.00

Birchgrey

A new promoter, a new beginning

David Cannon

The return to Sunningdale proved a master stroke -as this 1984 view shows - the crowds welcomed this major tournament on South West London's doorstep.

In the beginning, Swedish sporting hero Sven Tumba had an idea - a golf tournament to reflect the coming together of the golfing nations of Europe. It would be called, appropriately enough, the European Open and it became a reality. In 1978 at Walton Heath in Surrey, top players from Europe, augmented by a number of leading Americans, contested the first Championship.

Three years later the cost of staging the Championship was spiralling out of control. Tumba, who was not personally involved financially, had discreetly stepped out of the picture as the battle to keep his "baby" a viable operation, within the European Tour, began in earnest.

Tumba's idea had been a simple one - maybe too simple. Sponsors from various European countries would combine to promote the event each year. It would be ideal if the tournament were staged in a different European country each year but it was best to start in Britain and stay there until it was well established. Tumba's reputation ensured he received maximum support for the exciting venture from not only his Swedish friends but also the Finns who had become interested in golf and who, one day in the not too distant future, might have their own Open.

Yet in attempting to launch the tournament on a grand scale, the organisers ended up paying out much more than they earned. The idea was a good one - making it

work was much more difficult. Tumba, along with Ruene Ericsson, had enlisted support in the early days from Jaakko Pöyry, the Finnish consulting engineers, and the Finnish conglomerate Nokia, whose business is in electronics, plastics and rubber products. The original plan had been to have about eight sponsors. There never were. Also, appearance fees for the visiting Americans, for instance, were crippling. In April 1981, just four months away from the date of the fourth European Open at Royal Liverpool Golf Club, Hoylake, the future of the event, with a projected loss to creditors of £140,000 and to sponsors of very much more, was hanging perilously in the balance.

As the storm clouds gathered over the seriously troubled event, a plan based upon the then current information (which later proved to be incorrect) to save the tournament was formulated by Manne Ehrstrom, finance director of Pöyry who had enlisted the help of Clarkson Puckle, Lloyds Insurance Brokers of London.

The plan was for Nokia, Pöyry and Clarksons each to put in £20,000 of capital and give the newly formed company a £20,000 loan. This would eliminate effectively the money owed the creditors, although in effect it did not. Some creditors who had given up hope of getting their money back re-appeared on the scene when the rescue package was launched and the overall deficit in this area turned out to be more than double the original figure - well over £300,000.

Why, you might ask, did Nokia, Pöyry and Clarksons not just throw in the towel and cut their considerable losses?

The answer is simple enough. All *believed* in the European Open as much as Tumba had three years earlier. The battle to save the event and all it stood for, began in earnest on a pleasant evening in April in the City of London, or to be more exact, at the Ibex House headquarters, in The Minories, of Clarksons. Clarksons and Pöyry were directly involved in it but not Nokia. There, at the important gathering, was Ken Schofield, chief executive of the PGA European Tour who had a vested interest in wanting the event to continue and succeed. The discussion lasted for four hours from five o'clock and ended with agreement on the proposed rescue package.

Hands were shaken on the understanding that as a quid pro quo for Clarksons, Nokia and Pöyry putting their faith in the event into tangible financial support, the Tour should reciprocate by sharing in the financial responsibility on similar terms. Ken Schofield agreed in principle but later had to tell the new company that constitutionally he was unable to do so. He had a plan, however, which he hoped would solve the problem. Someone would stand nominee for the PGA. That someone was Peter Urwin. With the tournament deadline approaching fast, the new group, operating under the "off-the-shelf" title of Birchgrey Ltd had inherited the organisation left by Tumba as well as the debts of creditors but they decided to accept Schofield's alternative plan and stay in.

Although there was no concrete reason why they should, the men involved in the new company believed, at first, that Peter Urwin was a PGA person. In fact he was simply a friend of Ken Schofield who had asked, two years earlier, [as they played round in a competition organised at Walton Heath) whether there was anything he could do to involve himself more closely with the tour. Urwin, involved in the exporting of educational and scientific equipment to Africa and with property interests, played off 4 at Roehampton and was still a member at Sierra Leone where he had been captain. He loved his golf.

"I wondered if I could sponsor a young lad on Tour with a view, I suppose, to becoming more involved in the weekly pro-ams," admits Urwin who had watched the first European Open at Walton Heath in 1978 as a spectator. "I lived near the course at that time and just went along out of interest. I never for a moment thought that one day I might be responsible for its organisation.

After Urwin's initial enquiry not much happened, certainly not quickly. He and Schofield met several times at golf outings but in 1981 he received the call that was to change the whole direction of his life and involve him far more closely in golf than ever before.

Schofield asked whether he would be prepared to underwrite the PGA share of the contract which had been drawn up to save the European Open – £20,000 in cash and a £20,000 loan. Peter gave it some thought and agreed. The final piece of the jigsaw had been completed and the recovery process would begin in earnest.

Ian Crawford-Smith, of Clarksons, believed in those days that Peter Urwin's role was simply to be the "eyes and ears" of the Tour on the new company board. Urwin's initial involvement was slight, except that being the only person on the Board, now working to re-establish the European Open who knew anything about golf, he became closely involved in 1981 with the last-minute negotiations that enabled Severiano Ballesteros to return to the circuit after his damaging six-month absence while in dispute about appearance money. The Tour had agreed a $10,000 limit on expenses (appearance money by another name). Seve accepted the situation and, hopeful of making the Ryder Cup later in the year, returned to the fold. He would not be invited to play in the Cup match but he did wonders for the European Open!

Seve's comeback in the Championship he has never missed, seemed in a way to have justified all the hectic behind-the-scenes activity of the unlikely four men now locked together to turn the loss-making event into a profitable business investment. In fact the recovery programme would take over eight years but no one knew that in the late summer of 1981 . . . and maybe just as well! Among the first actions of the new board had been to enlist the help of consultants to urgently try and find a main sponsor. There had been too little time left for any real hope of finding one for 1981 and the board realised this. So an "in-house" solution was devised with the help of Kenneth Kemp, the chairman of Smith and Nephew who owned 50 per cent of British Tissues, the makers of, amongst other products, Dixcel toilet tissue. The other 50 per cent of British Tissues was owned by Nokia, one of the shareholders in Birchgrey.

In fact, there were only three shareholders by now. When the decision had been taken to carry on it had been decided to negotiate a major loan from the shareholders. Nokia, Pöyry and Clarksons agreed. Peter Urwin, for obvious reasons, was not in a position to provide this kind of money. He was bought out but was poised, nevertheless, to play an even more important role in the operation.

That infusion of money from those companies involved in Birchgrey had ensured that the 1981 event showed an operating profit of £20,000 but hopes that a new sponsor would be found for the 1982 event were not to be realised, despite the fact that with Ken Schofield's help the impressive Sunningdale course in Surrey had agreed to take the Championship - a partnership that was to last five important solidifying years. Sunningdale remains the venue every second year.

Sunningdale gave the Championship extra status. The course is recognised as one of the best inland courses in the country and has always been a favourite with professionals from all over the world. The decision to go there was another stroke of genius which helped the rebuilding of the tournament's dented prestige.

The selling of corporate hospitality packages had been stepped up and having moved from a relatively depressed area in terms of commerce and business to the comfortable south-east, it meant that this part of the business expanded. Instead of ten hospitality tents as had been the case at Hoylake, there were 30 at Sunningdale, but still no main sponsor. It was proving much more difficult than the Birchgrey board imagined, to lure a big money sponsor to give the financial operation a necessary boost. There was considerable interest but no commitment. This time Clarksons were named as main sponsor after a fruitless search by West Nally and the enthusiastic work behind the scenes of tournament organiser Roseanne Arnell who had also been involved in the early tournaments as well.

"We believed there really was a sponsor round the corner just waiting to come in and join up and this kept us going," says Ian Crawford-Smith. "It was an immense act of faith on our part or sheer stupidity or a combination of both but we stayed with the project refusing to admit defeat, still convinced we owned what would eventually become a viable operation." By 1982 Urwin had been given a new role. He had been made Managing Director of the company which had moved into new premises near Urwin's home in Wimbledon. They were still paying off creditors, with the smaller suppliers among the most determined to be paid out in full. Programmes were impounded, car park money held back, but eventually the records showed that the creditors had been satisfied. The 1982 Championship, however, lost £30,000. Significantly every one since has shown a profit.

Things were moving in the right direction but problems continued to crop up. When Birchgrey had taken over the running of the tournament they had been given the title by Ken Schofield with every justification. The previous owners of the title and organisers of the tournament had failed. Now with the event more successful again, Ruene Ericcson sued Birchgrey over his original agreement. The action was eventually dropped and another chapter in the chequered history of the event was over.

Peter Urwin would additionally take over the running of the event in 1983, following the departure of Roseanne Arnell but his main role in the Championship week of 1982 was to entertain prospective clients, people who might, with a little persuasion, be willing to produce the big money the tournament needed. Many companies were interested in what was now a highly successful promotion on the ground but the most significant conversation of that week involved Urwin and a young executive from the Panasonic electronics company. Miles Dawson was involved with the Japanese company's corporate sponsorship packages and had involved the company in one day's activities at the Bob Hope Classic at Moor Park. A keen golfer himself, Dawson had been invited along to have a look at the staging of the European Open after Birchgrey had heard on the grapevine that Panasonic were interested in becoming involved in golf in a bigger way.

Birchgrey wanted to sign up a company which was looking for a highly visible up-front advertising platform in a quality sport. That company would pick up a £200,000 sponsorship package with the remainder coming from a host of smaller sponsors (now called patrons) paying much less for the privilege of using the facilities at the European Open as a chance to entertain clients in pleasant surroundings.

In the case of the latter branch of sponsorship activity, Peter Urwin had enlisted the help, in 1983, of George Griffith whom he met, as he had Ken Schofield, on the golf course. Urwin, Griffith, John Simpson of the International Management Group and Jose-Maria Canizares were brought together in the State Express pro-am at The Belfry and, put simply, one thing led to another.

Griffith was involved with one of his clients who was sponsoring the driving range at the tournament that week. Urwin was impressed enough at what he had heard from Griffith. The result was the formation of a new company, Vantage, headed by Griffith, which is now heavily involved on the corporate hospitality side of the European Open. This year there are 150 corporate sponsors - fifteen times as many as there were in 1981, the first year of Birchgrey involvement.

Meanwhile, discussions continued in late 1982 to find that corporate sponsor willing to provide a six-figure involvement in the Championship. There were several potential clients but in the end the battle developed into a two-horse race between Panasonic and Miles Dawson and Benson and Hedges, whose Len Owen had shown a keen interest in assuming the overall sponsorship role.

In the end Panasonic signed first and it was Peter Urwin's sad task to travel to the Benson and Hedges headquarters, then at Kingsway, to break the news to an enthusiastic Silk Cut board, that a deal had already been struck with the Japanese company.

The partnership with Panasonic was further cemented as a result of a signing ceremony in a small office in Slough in early 1983 attended by Ken Schofield, Peter Urwin, Miles Dawson and Andy Imura, managing director and founder of Panasonic UK, when Panasonic guaranteed their involvement with the tournament through until 1990.

"We drank champagne that grey January day," recalls Peter Urwin. "As far as we were concerned, however, the sun was shining." The final piece of a complicated jigsaw had been fitted into place when Panasonic signed and the European Open was set for great things.

The Panasonic European Open is a success story now, but that success was achieved by taking hard decisions along the way and with a not inconsiderable reservoir of goodwill from a great many people in various branches of the game.

Most importantly, the Championship's success was the result of, quite simply, sheer hard work by the men and women who run Birchgrey and who might never have got together at all but for the convincing argument put up by Ken Schofield in defence of the event at that meeting in the City in the spring of '81.

There was every reason for the rescue operation to fail. Happily, it has turned out to be a magnificent triumph.

The latest twist in the Birchgrey saga has seen the departure of Clarksons as one of the shareholders. They had become Clarkson Puckle and then Bain Clarkson within the Inchcape organisation, and golf sponsorship did not fit into the new corporate plan. Now it is Nokia, Jaakko Pöyry and Peter Urwin, back in again with some of his Birchgrey colleagues, who are the shareholders.

The best that European golf had to offer could not stop Australian Greg Norman from winning the 1986 event at Sunningdale.

Ron Heager of the *Daily Express*

There was a hero's welcome for the return of Roberto de Vicenzo, the Argentinian winner of the Open at Hoylake in 1967.

The 1981 European Open was the one which very nearly did not take place. Only an inspired rescue act masterminded by European Tour executive director Ken Schofield with the invaluable assistance of Peter Urwin of Birchgrey, enabled it to be staged at all. Yet in the end it provided a classic winner in Graham Marsh – an Australian whose only disappointment in the game must surely have been never to have won an Open. The way he played the demanding Royal Liverpool Championship course at Hoylake in the 1981 European Open only highlighted how well he could cope with seaside links playing at their toughest with hard, bouncy, sun-baked fairways. Taking the European title was some consolation to the former schoolteacher for his failure to win a major and with the tournament having grown in prestige his victory at Royal Liverpool is standing out ever more impressively on his long list of successes around the world.

The late Ron Heager of the *Daily Express* and *Sunday Express* captured the on-course drama that year and it had to be good to outshine all the tension and anxiety of events behind the scenes in the months leading up to the Dixcel sponsored Championship. This was how he reported the golf in 1981:

Those masters of the art of collecting important golf titles, Jack Nicklaus and Tom Watson, have over the years amply demonstrated there is more to winning championships than filing an entry, making a date in the diary, boarding a jet and arriving punctually on the tee.

Their golfing year is planned around their major targets. Planned in meticulous detail are other tournament appearances, travel to the theatre of operations, practice schedules, even practice times. Reflecting on the 1981 European Open Championship prompted these thoughts, because there was marked contrast in the immediate preparations for the championship among the three players who turned out to be the principal protagonists.

One came jet-lagged from the World Series of Golf in America, in the midst of a travel schedule rivalling the peripatetic wanderings of Gary Player. A second arrived from the beaches of his native land, considerably undergolfed because of a self-imposed boycott of the European Tour. The third made the long haul from Kalgoorlie in Western Australia to ease himself gently from Pacific to British Summer Time in the stands at The Oval, viewing the final England-Australia Test.

Which proved the winning formula? History tells us that it was cricket buff Graham Marsh who got it right. He had the mental reserve to produce his most telling golf shots in the final round.

The high-flying Greg Norman, pushing mind and body to the limits, made the pace with a first-round record 66 on the venerable links of the Royal Liverpool Club at Hoylake. But he

woke from his jet trance to reality. The cutting edge of sharp scoring was blunted. He finished four strokes back, joint third to Marsh.

The second hero of the tournament was the glamorous Spaniard, Severiano Ballesteros. Seemingly unaffected by the train of controversy his season had brought, he added a second 68 to his name to take the lead.

This was his return to the European fold after wrangles over appearance money. He had not played since the US PGA Championship a month earlier. He was left out of the Ryder Cup team. He appeared unscarred. Blandly he brushed aside the prickly points of the recent past. He needed success because, "My prestige

is low". And that looked completely within his grasp, on a still defenceless Hoylake - sunbaked and fast running, windless and with those superb greens - he shot 67 and stretched his lead to four strokes from Marsh and Ireland's Des Smyth on the third day.

As in any well-constructed drama, the final act produced a surprise twist to the plot. The perfectly tuned Marsh did all the things Seve is supposed to do.

Marsh made par when the Spaniard was in two bunkers and took a double bogey at the fifth. Two shots gained. Marsh eagled the 8th against Seve's par.

That four-stroke lead had gone. Marsh

The historic Hoylake course at Royal Liverpool was an excellent venue for the first Birchgrey promoted European Open.

David Cannon

Fourth European Open

holed a 12 feet saving putt for his par at 12 and salvaged a par from the hay at 14, where Seve missed a gift birdie putt.

Then "tiger" Marsh pulled out his decisive stroke. He rolled in a putt of 25 yards from the front of the terraced 15th green for a birdie while Ballesteros drove into the rough and could do no better than a bogey. This was the crucial two-shot swing.

Marsh played the feared 16th across the corner of the practice field in the manner of Roberto de Vicenzo in his memorable 1967 Open victory - driver, 3-wood . . . birdie. And when danger threatened from a bunkered drive at 17 Marsh quelled it with a 6-yard putt to save par and preserve his two-stroke lead as Seve missed an 8 feet birdie chance.

Hoylake, in any condition, is renowned for the severity of its five finishing holes. The par is 5, 4, 5, 4, 4. Matching these 22 strokes, it is said will win a championship in the final count. Marsh, with a raw ferocity belied by his urbane, friendly personality, played the holes in 20. So the generally laid-back, shrewdly paced approach of globetrotter Marsh prevailed over the non-stop Norman and stay-at-home Ballesteros.

Marsh's battle honours at Hoylake were won not only by the dagger thrusts of his last round 68 - against Seve's 74 - for he had a running feud with the old links from the opening day. A first nine holes of 37 did not threaten to win any championship. He came back in 30. Next day he was out in 33. Hoylake showed its distaste for such treatment. The back nine cost him 39 strokes - nine up on the previous day!

Life was like that in European Open week at Royal Liverpool. With splendid imagery, Peter Dobereiner in his *Guardian* report likened Hoylake to an irate Victorian merchant who retaliated against would-be muggers by laying about with his malacca cane. After Christy O'Connor, jun, had equalled Norman's record 66 on the second day he paid for his temerity with a 77 and 72.

Bernard Gallacher was one stroke off the lead after his part in the sub-par scoring spree in the two opening rounds. Next day Hoylake's out of bounds twice snared him into a 73. The third round saw the emergence of the mugger-of-the-week in the unlikely person of Brian Waites with a new record of 64. And that began with a five at the first, so he played 17 holes in nine under par. The members were just recovering from this mid-afternoon outrage when Seve Ballesteros steamed in with four birdies in the last five holes for a 67 and a four-stroke lead as the encore to his two eagles of the second round. But the illustrious Latin paid the price as he was overtaken in the final run-in.

To date Seve has still not won the European Open. He needs this title, the Italian and Portuguese Opens to complete his grand slams of European Open Championships.

At the age of 68, Argentinian Roberto de Vicenzo returned to the scene of his 1967 Open triumph, was delighted to be made an honorary member of the club where after twenty years of trying he had finally won a major, and then held his own for two rounds with Severiano Ballesteros and Sam Torrance. Roberto shot 74, 71, made the cut by two shots and in the end finished on 289 - one over par on the course that had provided one of the greatest moments of his golfing life. There had been tears running down his sun-tanned cheeks after his popular success in 1967 when, no doubt still in a state of shock at his triumph, he left the trophy behind. He must have noticed the contrasts the passage of fourteen years can bring. In 1967 the qualifying cut was 149, with 58 players making it. This time it was 147, with 75 going through. And remember they were playing the big ball. Total prize-money in Vicenzo's Open was £15,000. The Dixcel European Open winner took home £17,500 out of a total prize fund of £105,000.

Marsh took the title but Greg Norman, early in his career, made headlines, too, revealing how he coped with jet-lag! In the middle of a seven-week travel stint involving 50,000 miles he admitted he had taken a tip from Gary Player, the world's most experienced commuter! Said Greg: "His recipe is a simple one. He told me he always drinks several pints of water before boarding a jet, to combat dehydration, then a sleeping tablet before curling up on the carpet and sleeping from take off to touch down.

"I try to do the same - it's the only way to beat jet-lag."

Seve had been in dispute all season regarding appearance money but he wasted no time in hitting top form on his return.

Portrait of a Winner
Marsh

Renton Laidlaw of *The Evening Standard*

Phil Sheldon

A lucky spectator about to receive the winning ball which a delighted Australian Graham Marsh used in his closing title-winning round at Hoylake.

Gary Player, in a new book published recently, suggested that he had travelled so much to keep golfing dates that he had in effect already been round the world 54 times. Australian Graham Marsh who won the 1981 Dixcel European Open at Royal Liverpool might not be far behind that figure now and might even have passed it by the time he is 52 in eight years time.

Marsh and his family – wife Julie Marie and children Tony, Jennifer, Jeremy and young Stephanie – live in Perth, Western Australia, but from the moment he decided to quit selling insurance to play golf full-time, he has been on the move. He really does follow the "have clubs, will travel" syndrome but then that was inevitable from his

somewhat remote base. Born on 14 January 1944 in Kalgoorlie, Graham Marsh has played and won on all the major circuits in the world – his own Australian-New Zealand circuit, of course, but also regularly in Japan, often in Europe and once when he played the American circuit for three years. In 1977, at the age of 33, golfing globetrotter Marsh won the Sea Pines Heritage Classic in South Carolina, an event which has since been won by other foreigners on the US circuit – Nick Faldo and Bernhard Langer. The amusing thing in Marsh's case was that his Sea Pines win helped him collect a rather unusual award that year in the States. He ended up, because he fulfilled all the requirements, as Rookie of the Year – an old one – but still the best newcomer that season.

He has a natural wanderlust, however, and playing on the world stage, he found, was more to his liking than concentrating on the American Tour even if it is the richest in the world. One hotel room looks like another in the States. He felt hemmed in. He could not be guaranteed releases to play where he wanted to when he wanted to. He needed more air so, having proved a point notably to himself, he quit America to resume his global and, at times, punishing schedule, but then Graham Marsh has never been afraid of hard work. Sport was a high priority in the family household when Graham was a child. His younger and more extrovert brother Rodney became an Australian Test cricketer with an ability to knock up the runs in a crisis. Rodney is a wicketkeeper and as youngsters he and Graham, no doubt, played cricket together. Indeed but for an accident Graham might have ended playing cricket for a living, too, instead of golf. Cricket is everything in Australia. Losing the Ashes to England is a national disaster. Playing for your country is the ultimate but Graham, who was an opening bat in his State Schools side, hitting runs rather faster than Geoffrey Boycott, opted for golf after breaking his left arm and being unable to play cricket for a time.

"The arm was in plaster and in order to keep exercising it and strengthening it I started swinging a golf club and was hooked," he recalls. Not that he had thoughts, at that time, of making his career from a game that stylish Australian Peter Thomson had been enhancing around the world. It was just after that period in Australian golfing history when the "Melbourne Tiger" was hardly ever out of the frame in the Open Championship and Kel Nagle was impressing internationally too – notably at St Andrews in 1960 when he won the Centenary Open and in the process pipped Arnold Palmer by one shot. The significance of that was that Palmer was on a Grand Slam bid that year having won the US Masters and US Open. Australian golf's reputation, thanks mainly to what these two great ambassadors were doing, was high.

Studious Marsh, however, took a cautious role as far as his early career was concerned. Today he may spend hours of his life in planes and airports but initially he stayed put in Perth teaching mathematics at a local school for three and a half years. It was all reasonably mundane. He enjoyed his job but when he was posted to a country school and realised it would affect his amateur playing schedule, Marsh turned insurance salesman. When that gradually began to pall, Marsh gambled on golf. In 1968 at the age of 24 he turned professional and two years later in New Zealand won the first of over 50 victories by taking first prize in the now defunct Watties tournament.

It has long been the case that Australian players gravitated naturally to Europe during their winter 'down-under' to continue their golfing careers and from 1970 Marsh has been coming – sometimes for a lengthy period, sometimes for just a handful of tournaments to Europe. He has not missed coming one year. Today his schedule is a necessarily tight one in order that he can fit in his Japanese Tour commitments – financially so important to him. He has become an integral part of the Japanese scene, one which is, traditionally, difficult to break into. Marsh has, over the years, won more than 20 events in Japan and is as highly respected there as he is in Europe. His last

Graham Marsh gave himself time to acclimatise to British conditions and his pre-European Open preparation paid off.

win in Japan was the Taiheyo Masters in November of 1987 when he beat Tom Watson by a shot. A British colleague from the press corps was reporting the tournament and you can imagine his initial surprise and chagrin when the Australian conducted the whole winner's interview in fluent Japanese! Marsh can consider himself a pioneer in Japan, playing, as he has, since before they started keeping circuit records in 1974. He has won there the staggering sum of 360 million yen – which represents a large slice of the total of over 3 million US dollars he has banked during his successful career.

Marsh may have been a comparatively late starter in golfing terms and, as a result, have had to put a very firm emphasis, in the early days, on making a living rather than achieving major titles, but he has passed two of the goals he set himself when he started out almost twenty years ago. He easily made his million and with 55 victories to his name achieved another of his early aspirations. Not too many people do win that number of events. Few if any do so on four continents.

His third great hope was to win the Open. It is a disappointment to him that he has failed so far. He has not yet given up hope that he still might do so, even if he is now 44, but is realistic enough to appreciate how much keener the competition is today. "I failed by two shots to win in 1975 at Carnoustie and again by two at Birkdale in 1983," says Marsh who plans on keeping himself competitively sharp – health permitting – to be successful on the American Seniors' circuit for which he qualifies as a result of the Sea Pines victory on the main Tour eleven years earlier.

He plays these days around 26 tournaments a year – fewer than he once did but deliberately in order to let him devote time to his other interests. He has always believed he had far more capacity in him than just playing golf and is proving that now. He also enjoys involving himself in television commentary but has no plans to write an instruction book like everyone else it seems! That kind of thing bores him. "Someone once told me that the only golf books that sell are instructional manuals and I am not interested in doing that," says the golfer who was awarded the MBE in 1985 for his services to the game.

He was chairman of the Australian PGA from its inception in 1978 and although he stepped down three years ago for Terry Gale to take over, Marsh is still a strong voice on the executive committee. Australia has not proved an easy country in which to co-ordinate the golfing operation with so many different bodies and organisations pulling in opposite directions, but Marsh believes that by hanging out for what he thinks is best for the development of the game, they have won through. There are more good golfers coming out of Australia than ever these days and that, he feels, is the reward for not buckling under to the pressures exerted on those running the circuit by others with more independent and selfish views – views which he considers not in the best interests of the sport.

The current situation has not been achieved without a certain amount of personal pain. His popularity in Australia is probably less there than in any of the other countries in which he plays. It is a price he is prepared to pay for what he considers a just cause. He has shown the same fighting qualities off the course as he has shown on them over the years and now he is building courses too. Along with his partner Ross Watson, Marsh's company has thirteen in the pipe-line, half of them in Japan where building courses requires considerable engineering skill. Their flagship course, however, is currently in Australia appropriately enough at his base in Perth. It is a 27-hole complex called The Vines and has met with considerable independent acclaim.

Marsh, also involved in club design and manufacture with Prosimmon, is certainly not slowing down. He is sensible enough, however, to give himself time to devote to each of his interests. It means he never gets bored and, as he also admits to enjoying travelling, we can expect to see him around for many years to come.

September 3-6, 1981
Royal Liverpool G.C., Hoylake.

Prize money; £105,000
Par out: 36, Par in: 36, Yardage: 7,019

								£
1	Graham Marsh	Aus.	67	72	68	68	275	17,500.00
2	Severiano Ballesteros	Spa.	68	68	67	64	277	11,500.00
3	Nick Job	GB	71	70	69	69	279	4,388.75
	Sandy Lyle	GB	72	69	68	70	279	4,388.75
	Greg Norman	Aus.	66	71	71	71	279	4,388.75
	Brian Waites	GB	73	71	64	71	279	4,388.75
7	Des Smyth	Ire.	71	67	69	73	280	2,200.00
8	Ian Mosey	GB	76	67	68	71	282	1,950.00
9	Michael King	GB	71	71	72	69	283	1,575.00
	Bernhard Langer	Ger.	73	71	69	70	283	1,575.00
	Brian Barnes	GB	68	75	68	71	283	1,575.00
	Bernard Gallacher	GB	68	69	73	73	283	1,575.00
13	Rodger Davis	Aus.	71	72	69	72	284	1,400.00
14	Mark James	GB	69	73	77	66	285	1,300.00
	Nick Faldo	GB	71	74	69	71	285	1,300.00
	Vicente Fernandez	Arg.	69	71	73	72	285	1,300.00
15	John Morgan	GB	71	70	73	72	286	1,120.00
	John Bland	SA	72	68	74	72	286	1,120.00
	Harold Henning	SA	74	68	71	73	286	1,120.00
	Sam Torrance	GB	74	71	68	73	286	1,120.00
	Maurice Bembridge	GB	71	69	73	73	286	1,120.00

Gordon Richardson of *Golf Illustrated*

While it had been generally expected that the first Spaniard to win the title would be Severiano Ballesteros, it was another golfer from the Iberian peninsula who got his name on the trophy first – Manuel Pinero. He did it with all the craft we had come to expect from a European champion . . . as Gordon Richardson noted in his reports that week for *Golf Illustrated:*

Spaniard Manuel Pinero celebrated his thirtieth birthday six days late with a smash-and-grab victory worth £20,000 in the 1982 European Open at Sunningdale – and he did it in front of millions of his countrymen watching live on Spanish TV.

Little Manuel roared over the final nine holes in just 30 strokes (after turning five behind pacemaker Sam Torrance) for a course record 63 and a 14 below par 266. Scotland's Sam had looked sure of victory after romping out in 30 with three birdies in the first four holes and an eagle 2 at the 9th but came up two strokes short in the end. Sam finished with a 67 after dropping two strokes coming home as the pressure piled up to earn £13,320 and the ante post favourites Greg Norman (67) and Sandy Lyle (69), who could not buy a putt between them, shared third place two further back on 268, ten below par. Neil Coles charged to a closing 64 for fifth spot on 271.

It was quite a week for Pinero who had astonishingly failed to qualify for the last two rounds of the previous two European Opens and finished a modest 15th and 35th in the first two. This time he survived a bad joke after round three to make his challenge. Countryman Manuel Garcia 'pinched' his favourite wedge and for an anxious hour Manuel searched for it in vain. "When Manola produced it I was relieved, but also a little angry," confessed Pinero, whose luck on the greens after a lean summer was changed when one of the Sunningdale assistants loaned him his spare Ping putter.

Pinero explained: "That helped very much but the main reason I won was that I suddenly found my rhythm. It had come and gone all year, but I took two weeks off before·the Irish Open to practise. I went there full of confidence but the wind that week and at York made me lose it all again. Conditions at Sunningdale - no wind and nice and warm - made it possible for me to find my swing again and after I birdied nine and ten in the last round I knew I was going to win. My concentration was 100 per cent.

"But I was unhappy at not being in the last threeball after I had the best round of the third day. It meant that I was often distracted by the crowds coming up behind with Norman, Torrance and Lyle.

"It was marvellous to win when the play was being seen live on TV back home."

Peter Dazeley

Winner Pinero borrowed a Ping putter from the Sunningdale pro and it earned him a five figure birthday cheque.

Three from the edge at the short 13th and three putts at the 16th dashed Torrance's hopes of adding to his splendid Carroll's Irish Open victory of last year. The third day had been one of misses and might-have-beens. Torrance reckoned he had missed as many as six birdie chances inside 5 yards - yet he still shot 64 to match Norman's two-day-old course record to share the lead with Lyle who calculated he had missed five putts inside 5 feet in his 67.

Lyle, nine below par after birdie threes at the 11th and 12th was two ahead of Norman and three ahead of Torrance, but he fluffed a vital 4-footer for a two at the 13th, then three-putted the long 14th to waste a great birdie chance. Going out he had bungled an 18-inch putt to bogey the 6th and he was lucky to scramble par at the 17th after a miscued second shot ended 30 yards wide of the green - so wide, in fact, that he missed the real trouble.

Norman, though, probably suffered most on the greens after a bright start, in which he birdied three of the first five holes. He then three-putted the 6th and short 8th and chipped and three-putted the 9th for bogeys.

"I simply cannot get any touch on the greens - I've no idea of the speed. If I've got a downhiller I knock it 3 feet past and everything uphill I leave a foot short," he complained. So it was Torrance who stole the show on the third day after a dazzling eagle-birdie-birdie 3, 3, 3 start, which swept him out in 31. He picked up a penalty stroke after getting into a ditch at the 11th but added more birdies at 13, 14 and 16.

Sam had started out three behind Lyle and Norman (69) and Pinero, four behind the co-halfway leaders at the off, pulled up to joint second place with Torrance, two behind, with a fine 67. The second round had provided plenty of excitement, perhaps the two extremes being Tony Jacklin's 2, 3, 3 start, of which more later, and Sandown Park assistant, Peter Stow's twelve at the 18th, where he drove into a bunker, unwittingly moved his ball when removing a stone (one penalty shot), played it without replacing it (two more), then hit two in a row out of bounds on to the practice putting green.

Headline of the day, however, was "Worm catches Shark". A 6 inch earthworm popped its head out on the 7th tee just as

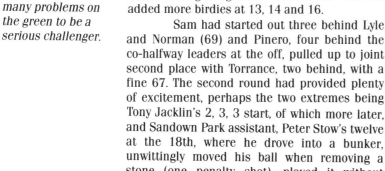

Sandy Lyle had too many problems on the green to be a serious challenger.

An outward 30 on the final day gave Sam Torrance a title chance - but he could not cope with Pinero's counter-attack on the last nine.

Norman ("Great White Shark") was on his back-swing and he cold-topped his ball about 20 yards into dense undergrowth to run up a double bogey. "I was so surprised I took my eye off the ball," confessed Greg, who slipped to a modest 70 and a 134 score, to be caught by Lyle, round in 66 for 134.

Norman's brilliant opening 64 had left the fans wondering "Who's going to be second?" With 32 strokes and 32 putts it compared favourably with Bobby Jones's 66 (33 and 33) in the Open qualifying over the course in 1926. Sadly he could not maintain this form, and

Fifth European Open

Severiano Ballesteros and his caddy, brother Vicente, check the figures - and find they do not match up to those of fellow Spaniard Manuel Pinero.

Peter Dazeley

sadly, too, a 'rusty' Severiano Ballesteros was out of it after an opening 72 left him eight off the lead.

Still Spanish pride was more than evident as the main prize went to Manuel Pinero, a man so often likened to Gary Player because of his size and 'heart' when under the severest pressure. Achieving something before Seve, has its own warm pleasure for any Spaniard. Manuel Pinero was happy that week at Sunningdale ... so was everyone who watched him win.

At the end of the week, Tony Jacklin was presented with a rare memento of a rare golfing feat which gave him the best start to a

tournament round he had achieved in his distinguished career - picking up five shots in the first three holes on the second day.

He started with a spectacular two on the Old course's par five first hole of 494 yards, after a perfect drive, followed by a 2-iron which he knew was going close - "but only realised it had gone into the hole when I heard the crowd cheering by the green," he said. It was the second albatross that Jacklin had achieved. Playing with Roberto de Vicenzo in the former Esso Round Robin event at Moor Park, he holed his second shot on the 504 yards 13th on the High course in the late 60s. After that spectacular start to his second round, Jacklin followed with birdies at the next two holes - holing from 25 feet and then from 6 feet but still shot 68. There was a surprise for him at the end of the tournament when he received an unexpected presentation - an American "double eagle" gold coin to celebrate his "double eagle", the US name for an albatross.

There has for long been talk of a match between Europe and Australia. The European Open provided a mini challenge before the real fireworks began. The two man Australian team of Greg Norman and Graham Marsh had to settle for a "Test" draw against Europeans Sandy Lyle and Bernhard Langer. But at the end of an 18-holes clash, it was the Aussies who beat Europe in the amount of cash won.

Birchgrey Ltd, promoters of the European Open, staged the challenge match for charity - with the Australians deciding to donate their share in a fourball match for £300 a hole to Cancer Research and Lyle and Langer deciding their share would go to the Golf Foundation. Though the match ended all square, the Australians claimed the major cash pay-out for their charity of £3,300 to the £2,100 which the European pair won.

"We felt the match would add a little spice to the occasion, following an outstanding Pro-Am, and the four stars were only too happy to join what proved to be an exciting curtain-raiser to the championship," said Peter Urwin, a director of Birchgrey Ltd. Norman rated the match as a worthwhile wind-up to his practice for the event - and it paid off for him with a first-round 64.

Pinero

Mitchell Platts of *The Times*

Manuel Pinero had been blown away at Dublin and York but the calmer conditions at Sunningdale helped him lift one of the most distinctive trophies in golf.

"It was the most emotional moment of my life," says Manuel Pinero. "Seve was crying his eyes out. We wrapped our arms around each other."

The place? Palm Springs, California. The event? The World Cup of Golf. The time? 1976. Ballesteros and Pinero had done for King and country what no Spaniards before them had achieved. Two ex-caddies each from unlikely backgrounds, had conquered the world. In retrospect it is, perhaps, the moment when America should have detected that their customary role as the proud overlords of the game was about to be challenged. Most certainly the Americans learned then to repect the lion-hearted Pinero. For there on the last green at Palm Springs it was Pinero, the son of a farm

foreman, who took the bull by the horns. He explained: "Seve and I both had putts from just short of 10 feet to win. Seve narrowly missed. It never crossed my mind that I wouldn't make mine. But when the ball dropped I was both relieved and ecstatic."

Pinero had yet to touch greatness. Yet the Americans once again fell victims to the little Spaniard's determined spirit as Europe won the Ryder Cup at The Belfry in 1985. Tony Jacklin, Europe's captain, was already indebted to the Ballesteros-Pinero partnership. They had linked again to win three points out of four as Europe edged 9-7 ahead. A famous victory was no more than a few hours away.

It was then that Jacklin played his trump card. He entrusted Pinero with the unenviable task of leading the expectant troops into battle on the Brabazon course.

That pitted Pinero against the terrier-like Lanny Wadkins. Jacklin was fully aware of the importance of that first confrontation. If the Spaniard won then a tidal wave of confidence would filter back through the entire team.

Pinero let neither Jacklin nor the team down. What is more the Americans were shattered by the news that Wadkins, whom they considered to be a banker, had been shredded 3 and 1 by the diminutive Spaniard. It was a performance which gave Pinero as much pleasure as his PGA Championship win in 1977. And not surprisingly, it left him as emotionally exhausted as did the Panasonic European Open at Sunningdale in 1982. Then he produced a record last round of 63, covering the last nine in an astonishing 30. That was another highlight in a remarkable story.

Pinero was born on 1 September 1952, in a humble hacienda on a farm close to the Spanish-Portuguese border town of Badahoz. His father came home that day, ripped open his wage packet and poured the contents on to the kitchen table. His reward for tending to 1,000 pigs was a penurious 18 pesetas! Yet even that seemed a fortune to Pinero senior when a few years later, after becoming self-employed, he found himself in a state of bankruptcy. In truth he was the victim of another man's greed. The countryside where the Pinero family lived produced the finest Spanish ham and Manuel's father used his experience to select the very best. Unfortunately the investment squeezed the family budget to a standstill when the man to whom he was selling the ham refused to pay up. There was no option for the peseta-less family but to move to Madrid where they had relatives with whom they could live.

Little could they have known then that it was a move which in time would transform Manuel's life. For the plot of land which the family purchased with the residue from the sale of their house in Badahoz was less than ten minutes from the Club de Campo golf course. There, as the rich got richer in Franco's Spain, Pinero became one of more than 100 caddies. Poverty had condemned him like so many other youngsters to carrying a bag of clubs in order to swell the family income.

As important to Manuel as the 75 pesetas he received for his eighteen holes on the course was the knowledge that he could also obtain an education at Club de Campo where they had a first-class caddie school. There the caddies attended class eight hours each day, excluding Sunday, and only left when they were required to work.

It was Manuel's father who first encouraged his son towards a career in golf. He regarded the sport more highly than football and he was delighted that it gave Manuel a passionate interest. Like so many fathers he was concerned that his son did not wander aimlessly around the streets,not that there was ever much chance of that!

Manuel sharpened his short game by putting, even chipping, on the carpet in the lounge of the house which the money he earned as a caddie had helped to build. What is more he began to show signs of possessing a talent for the sport. In the annual caddies competition he borrowed a set of clubs from a member for whom he regularly worked and finished 5th with a score of 67 over nine holes.

Pinero, playing here to the 18th at Sunningdale, began his golf career as a 75 pesetas-a-round caddy and now has career earnings of over £500,000 !

Every day in August, when the members left the steamy-hot city and the caddies were allowed on to the course, Manuel played from dawn to dusk. By 1967 he had graduated to the premier class in the caddie ranks and he finished third behind Jose-Maria Canizares in their championship. For his efforts in that event Pinero won a set of golf clubs. The next year he used them to win the caddies championship, and in 1969 he put together three sub-75 scores, passed

46

an examination on the rules of golf and opened the door to a career in the professional world.

Even so the importance of those years at the caddie school have never been lost on Pinero. He is concerned about the future because with the closing of the schools so the natural production line has disappeared. It needs the local authorities to make land available on which to develop municipal courses. No more has been heard, however, of the possibility of Ballesteros's company being offered two sites on the outskirts of Madrid to create such courses.

All of this frustrates Pinero for he has a deep affection for the game and a burning desire to ensure that as Spain plays host to an increasing number of tournaments, and to golfing holiday-makers, it is crucial not to ignore the Spanish youngsters' claims for places to play. Not that Pinero sees golf as a new sport for Spain because he insists that there is evidence to support the theory that his Spanish ancestors played a form of the game as early as the fourteenth century.

He explained: "I have found evidence in one village of wooden stakes being cut from trees and used to hit a wooden ball through the streets. In another game the boys of one village used trees as targets –hitting the ball from one to another with a club - to pass the time away."

The interest in the sport is gathering momentum because in one village close to Cordoba in the south the locals play with clubs made by the blacksmith. Similarly in Pozuelo, a suburb of Madrid where Pinero lives, the youngsters have laid out a home-made course using sand, which they rake flat, as the greens. There Pinero hopes in time to encourage the growth of a real course.

It is his way of trying to put something back into the sport because he is fully aware that without the assistance of others he, too, would never have clawed his way out of the poverty-stricken streets of Madrid to a respected place in the game of golf. What stifled Pinero's progress was the lack of funds with which to go out on to the growing European circuit and test his game against the finest exponents of the sport. That changed in 1972 when Patrick Edel, an executive with a petroleum company, agreed to sponsor him in return for receiving lessons.

It was a deal which transformed Pinero's career. Two years later he won his first important tournament in the city which had become his home. His confidence had increased with the winning of the Spanish PGA Championship in February 1974, and he now announced his arrival by winning the Madrid Open, against a full PGA European Tour field, at Puerto de Hierro.

Golf has made Manuel Pinero a very wealthy man, but it is a measure of his fascination for the game that the financial benefits dim in comparison with the fulfilment he has derived from his achievements.

He says: "This is the sport I love, the competition I enjoy. I never feel that my world is falling down if I play badly. I know that there will be another day, another week, another year."

September 2-5, 1982
Old Course, Sunningdale Golf Club, Berkshire.

Prize money; £120,000
Par out: 35, Par in: 35, Yardage: 6,563

								£
1	Manuel Pinero	Spa.	68	68	67	63	266	20,000.00
2	Sam Torrance	GB	67	70	64	67	268	13,320.00
3	Greg Norman	Aus.	64	70	69	67	270	6,760.00
	Sandy Lyle	GB	68	66	67	69	270	6,760.00
5	Neil Coles	GB	69	68	70	64	271	5,080.00
6	John Bland	SA	68	72	66	67	273	4,200.00
7	Vicente Fernandez	Arg.	70	71	69	66	276	3,300.00
	John O'Leary	Ire.	69	69	69	69	276	3,300.00
9	Rodger Davis	Aus.	69	67	74	67	277	2,540.00
	Nick Faldo	GB	70	72	67	68	277	2,540.00
11	Des Smyth	Ire.	71	69	70	68	278	2,025.00
	Christy O'Connor, jun.	Ire.	70	69	71	68	278	2,025.00
	Brian Waites	GB	68	72	69	69	278	2,025.00
	Manuel Calero	Spa.	68	69	71	70	278	2,025.00
15	Noel Ratcliffe	Aus.	70	71	72	66	279	1,720.00
	Graham Marsh	Aus.	68	70	71	70	279	1,720.00
17	Antonio Garrido	Spa.	73	68	71	68	280	1,560.00
	Paul Way	GB	72	70	69	69	280	1,560.00
	Ken Brown	GB	68	70	70	72	280	1,560.00
20	Maurice Bembridge	GB	72	69	70	70	281	1,480.00

Panasonic
Corporate Sponsors

Peter Urwin and Ken Schofield watch Ken Sakakibara sign the renewal of Panasonic's agreement, taking their sponsorship through to 1990.

Panasonic, main sponsors of the European Open since 1983, were attracted to golf sponsorship as a means of making the public more aware of a brand name change. Their association with the game and their high visibility during the European Open has done much good in helping the company, Matsushita, expand UK sales of a wide range of electronic products from a total of £193.5 million in 1983 to a projected £268 million in 1989. The company has moved a long way since Mr Konosuke Matsushita, now the executive adviser of the company, started a business with his wife and her brother to manufacture and sell a product of his own invention – a two-way lamp socket. This year Panasonic sponsored all video products to the Winter Olympics in Calgary and were sponsors to the Summer Olympics in Seoul – a commitment that ran into seven figures

Golf seemed an ideal vehicle for the company's sophisticated products. They represent quality and the sport has a reputation for fair play and honesty. In addition many of the people who follow golf were the potential customers of Panasonic. Initially the company involved itself in the Bob Hope Classic, a multi-sponsored national Pro-Am but although there was the offer of the Panasonic name being used in the full title of the tournament, the Panasonic board of directors decided that Bob Hope had too big a name with which to share top billing! The very real danger was that golf fans would continue to call the Bob Hope just that, so, when the chance came along to get involved in the European Open it seemed a much more attractive package. Sunningdale, too, was not far from the company's head office in Slough where the expansion of the product range had been masterminded for several years. The blend seemed irresistible. The company may be involved through their dealers in the sponsorship of basketball, yachting and, especially in France, of cycling but in Britain the main promotional vehicle is golf. At Sunningdale the Panasonic signs are maybe not everywhere but they are at strategic points, leaving no one in any doubt who is the sponsor.

Today over 1,800 people work for the Panasonic company, many of whose top customers are wined and dined at Sunningdale

in the luxurious hospitality marquees during the tournament. The European Open is, in fact, an extension of the company philosophy of putting something back into the community. In the European Open's case the company is providing entertainment but much of the company's community support scheme is educational, especially in engineering. Today Panasonic has 96 overseas facilities in 37 countries including 66 manufacturing companies. The total workforce is 170,000 of which 50,000 are in overseas establishments. It is a truly international operation and, as such, their golf involvement is international too. They sponsor events in America, Australia and in Europe, and Greg Norman has the distinction of having won all the tournaments with which they are

The sponsorship of Panasonic has ensured the ongoing success of the European Open. Here, Derrick Cooper competes in the 1987 Championship at Walton Heath.

David Cannon

involved. He won the Panasonic European Open in 1986, the year he won the Open, after beating Ken Brown in a play-off. That win earned him the £50,000 bonus that Birchgrey put up for anyone who can win both the European and Open Championships in the same year. Earlier in 1986 Norman had tied the US Tour record for 90 holes by shooting 333 at the Panasonic Las Vegas Invitational which has a prize fund of $1.14 million. Norman won $207,000 for that win but was disappointed not to break the scoring record. With the tournament won, he three-putted the last two greens!

In Australia in 1986 Greg led from start to finish to win the National Panasonic New South Wales Open and beat Terry Gale by a shot in the National Panasonic Western Australia Open. Last year he collected the National Panasonic Australian Open ahead of Sandy Lyle after a bizarre championship in which he walked off the course while playing the fourth round to speak to officials after he had called four times for them to come to him on the third tee. The problem was the wind – a 45 mph fierce north wind that made putting hazardous in normal conditions but impossible on the third green where the hole had been cut on a steep downslope. Several players complained but officials initially ignored the pleas until Norman made his protest. The round was abandoned but the "Great White Shark" took the title comfortably enough on one of his favourite courses the next day when he collected the first prize by ten shots.

Sunningdale

Alan Booth of *Golf Illustrated*

David Cannon

Severiano Ballesteros, still chasing his first European Open title, and Nick Faldo were both hoping for victory in the 1983 Championship, sponsored for the first time by Panasonic, to strengthen their claims for No. 1 spot on the money list but in the end they both finished in the pack behind the only Japanese golfer to win a British tournament. Isao Aoki, who had won the World Match Play title at Wentworth five years earlier found the Sunningdale course, just a little further down the A30 from London, equally to his liking as Gordon Richardson and Alan Booth reported in *Golf Illustrated*. Aoki led from start to finish:

Soothing daily massage from his pretty wife, Chie, eased the back pains of Isao Aoki and enabled him to snatch a £23,330 Panasonic European Open victory at windswept Sunningdale.

But a two-stroke win by the 6ft Japanese left European No. 1 Nick Faldo with a king-sized headache. After sharing the overnight lead with Aoki at five under par, following a third-round 68, to boost his hopes of becoming only the second British winner of the event after Sandy Lyle in 1979, and of becoming the first man since Bernard Hunt in 1963 to win five tournaments in a European season, as well as the first to top £100,000 prize-winnings in a season, Faldo slipped to a 71 and had to settle for joint second place with Carl Mason (68) and Severiano Ballesteros, who fired 64.

Their £10,440 left Faldo (£94,650) only £19,408 ahead of Ballesteros - hence Nick's dilemma. "I'd planned to by-pass the Swiss Open, so I could be best man at a wedding, but Seve is playing in Crans and can pass me at the top of the money if he wins," explained 26-year-old Nick. "It looks as if the money list is between me and him and I feel I must go wherever he goes," he said.

Nick spent 45 minutes after the prize-giving talking with his business manager John Simpson and PGA European Tour Executive Director Ken Schofield about the implications, mindful, no doubt, of the fringe benefits - put at several thousand pounds - if he stayed European No. 1. He went home to sleep on it, then decided: "I've got to play in Switzerland."

Nick Faldo came second, then decided he could not miss the Swiss Open if he wanted to be sure of finishing top money earner.

Once again Seve Ballesteros was left looking for that elusive European Open win despite a closing 64.

David Cannon

Faldo, ironically, might have had no problems. Ballesteros almost withdrew from the Sunningdale event during the second round because of a chest infection. Seve explained: "I came very, very close to pulling out. You'll never know how bad I felt. I could hardly breathe. But I took penicillin to cure the infection and it got a little better."

The infection was the result of a dramatic rescue Seve was involved in just days before the European Open began, when he and his brother Vicente saved a girl's life in the Spanish floods. After a nightmare drive through the floods, which devastated Northern Spain, the brothers finally managed to reach the 20-year-old girl, who suffered from kidney trouble, and drove her to hospital for crucial treatment. The brothers twice had to get out and push their Range Rover through waist-high water when the Santander floods, which killed 29 people, were at their worst. Seve kept his rescue mission secret, but the news leaked out at the European Open, where Seve said modestly: "It was nothing". He refused to blame the incident for his rather indifferent form.

"My game was not good either, but American Larry Nelson tried to help me. he was like a doctor telling me what was wrong, but not telling me the cure. Then I found out my shoulders were in the wrong place and, I think, on the last day I found my old swing again."

Aoki, who holed a 130-yard wedge shot to take the Hawaiian Open earlier in the year, becoming the first Japanese winner on the US circuit, arrived in Britain with a back injury, but his wife's daily massage eased away the pain and he had rounds of 65, 70, 70, 69 for a six-under-par 274 total.

He led all the way - by a shot from Ewen Murray and wealthy Sunningdale amateur Craig Francis, son of the late Frances Francis, international golfer, horseman and athlete of the 20s and 30s, on day one and by the same margin on day two from John Bland, Michael King and Canada's Jerry Anderson, with US Open Champion Nelson and Scot Bernard Gallacher among those failing to make the 144 qualifying mark. Victory was a perfect birthday present for Isao, 41 on the eve of the tournament. His famous "toe-up" putting style had earned him 39 Japanese titles. While Faldo was flagging, Mason, who started the week in 48th place in the money list, was producing his best performance of the season, more than doubling his prize winnings to almost £20,000.

Australian Greg Norman at last showed glimpses of his old form with a final round 66 for joint fourth place on 277 with Sam Torrance (68), whose £5,415 prize pushed his total winnings to £31,369 and made virtually certain of his Ryder Cup place. The man who forced Sam into second place in the 1982 event, Manuel Pinero, played with Ballesteros, closed with a 65 to finish joint seventh on 278 with Benson & Hedges winner John Bland, of South Africa, and Jose Maria Canizares. Pinero earned £3,610 and moved into the Ryder Cup top twelve with two qualifying events to go with £26,590 - at the expense of Ireland's Eamonn Darcy, forced to pull out after jarring his hand during a third round 84.

There were problems too, for another Irishman — the ex-Walker Cup player Philip Walton, who had turned professional only two months earlier. He had his adventures at Sunningdale, especially on the back nine. On the first day he completed the outward half in three over par 38 and hit trouble at the 10th taking a four over par 8. But worse was to come. As he reached the 17th he was ten over par and his chances of qualifying for the last two days were remote. After the 17th they had gone completely

They don't always agree, but at Sunningdale Greg Norman and Graham Marsh were the best of chums.

Sixth European Open

Isao Aoki shows his putting style, 1983 vintage.

– for he took a seven over par 11. Walton was just over the back of the green with his second shot and putted the ball down to three feet. After that he took six more putts, knocking the ball one handed with some of them and on the last putt hit the ball as it was moving and incurred a two stroke penalty.

Afterwards Walton said: "I just lost my head. No one should be on the course ten over par at that stage. I would have walked in except for the fact that it would have been unfair to my partners."

There was disappointment too, for Welshman Ian Woosnam who had an ace in his opening 69. Sadly it brought him no reward. He holed his 5-iron tee shot at the 182 yards 8th hole. If he had scored his ace at the 185 yards 13th he would have won a national Panasonic 45-inch screen back projection TV valued at £2,500. Seve Ballesteros did not leave Sunningdale without a title! He showed his skill on Sunningdale's putting green the day before the event to win the Panasonic Putting Championship from seven other players.

Ballesteros and Isao Aoki took part at the invitation of the sponsors, the other challengers being Bob Charles and Carl Mason, chosen from the 1982 PGA Putting Statistics and Manuel Pinero, Tom Sieckmann, Mike Cahill and Peter Teravainan from the 1983 statistics.

Ballesteros, as eager to win as if he were competing a major tournament, crushed Mason six and five in the 18-hole opening match, but then met stiffer opposition against countryman Manuel Pinero, who had earlier disposed of Cahill by one hole. Seve beat Peter Teravainan in the final. Ballesteros was not so lucky when, with Pinero, he competed in an 18-hole challenge match over the Old course, being beaten four and three by Americans Larry Nelson and Corey Pavin, winner of the German Open in July nor did he have any luck in the Championship which had produced no shortage of talking points!

So Aoki went back to Japan a happy man. Faldo went to Switzerland (and did end up top money earner that year by a healthy £67,000 over Ballesteros) and main sponsors Panasonic were delighted with their winner who ensured extensive television coverage back in Japan.

Portrait of a Winner
Aoki

Renton Laidlaw of *The Evening Standard*

Putting is a highly distinctive part of the game. There are those golfers with touch and feel who you could argue, could hole out with whatever they happened to be holding at the time. It is such a unique aspect of the game that it is a very indistinct science. The fact is, however, that there are great putters, average putters and golfers who go through their whole careers hitting superb shots through the green only to become quite histrionic on the putting surfaces. It so happens the 1983 Panasonic European Open winner Isao Aoki comes into the first category. He is a great putter and because he also happens to be one of the game's internationally respected iron-players too, it is no surprise that he has been Japan's most successful international performer over the years and still commands everyone's admiration.

Like Severiano Ballesteros he began his golfing life as a caddy at Abiko Club not far from the school he was attending. Always a tall boy for his age he was nicknamed "The Tower" by those at the club because he dwarfed all the other eager young bag carriers. Little did the members of the club realise that their nickname would, in the end, aptly describe him with regard to putting Japan on the international golfing map. He had been a giant, an always well-mannered, well turned out, stylishly dressed ambassador from a country where golf reigns supreme.

When he was a teenager Aoki was so caught up in the game that he would practise in the very early morning and again in the late evening, when no one was around, to perfect his shots. He was always good around and on the greens and it was expected he would make a quick breakthrough on the expanding Japanese

David Cannon

Isao Aoki has a unique putting style but it works like a charm as he proved at Sunningdale.

53

Sixth European Open

circuit when he turned professional in 1964 – the year the World Match Play title was inaugurated at Wentworth. In fact, Aoki went seven long, frustrating years before he stepped on to the dais to pick up a first prize cheque but he has made up for his somewhat tardy start. The six-footer with such a limited knowledge of English that he still uses an interpreter from time to time, has now won over 50 titles including one in the United States, and in this respect he is unique in Japanese golfing history.

His win in the States was achieved in the most spectacular fashion and if the "victim" of one of the best yet cruellest strokes in golf, slender Jack Renner, felt like weeping afterwards no one would have questioned his actions at all. The place where Aoki hit a shot which was heard around the world, was Waialae Country Club, venue of the 1983 Hawaian Open just several months before the European Championship. Picture the scene. Garlanded spectators round the last green were praising Jack Renner's performance. The beanpole American whose trade mark is his white Ben Hogan-style cap had just shot a 19-under-par total of 269. Back in the Press tent the reporters were preparing their stories congratulating Renner on his third career win. Nobody could catch him. The last group were coming down the last and technically Aoki could tie him if he made a birdie, but the Japanese player was in the longish rough grass in two at the par 5 hole. He would do well to get it on the green. A birdie from where he was seemed unlikely in the extreme!

Renner, concentrating on making sure the figures on his card were correct, looked unperturbed when suddenly from the green behind him came the most almighty roar. Aoki had done the impossible. He had pulled out his wedge and sunk his shot for a winning eagle. The ball flew 128 yards into the hole and Renner, instead of winning, had to be content with second place. Victory gave Aoki the greatest thrill of his life at that time. Winning the World Match Play in 1978 and the European in 1983 delighted him in some respects but nothing is sweeter to a

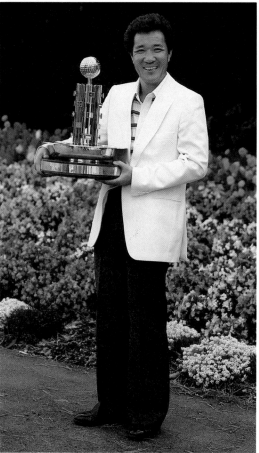

David Cannon

Champion Isao Aoki proudly wearing his European Open blazer – and with a Japanese winner Panasonic were delighted.

foreigner on the American circuit than to beat them at their own game. No other Japanese golfer has done that.

Mind you, there was one win which was probably more satisfying than even that and it, too, occurred in 1983 back in his native Japan. Four times he had been runner up in his national championship – the Japanese Open. In 1983 he finally won it and just to underline it was certainly no fluke he won the Japanese title again last year. It is that event that prevents him being at Sunningdale to try again for the European crown. His huge commitment in Japan, where the season stretches even longer than the European one, has prevented him playing more regularly in the States and seriously limited his visits to Britain, but he is an international jet-setter unlike so many of his younger rivals who are content to play for yen back home.

No one has won as many tournaments in Japan than Aoki however, who, it is said, adopted his peculiar putting technique purely by chance. In the early days he was scheduled to play an exhibition round but his clubs went missing. He had to borrow a set and they were the wrong size shaft. He had two options – to lay the club squarely on the ground and as a result have his body and arms in such a position that he might not be able to hit the ball, or stand further away and tilt the toe-end of the club upwards off the ground. It seemed bizarre but the talented Aoki made it work so effectively that he has maintained the unusual style throughout his career. Today on the greens the end of the putter blade is tilted crazily upwards. Aoki just picks up the big money time after time and goes smiling to his Japanese bank.

No Japanese golfer has ever won a major but Aoki came desperately close in 1980, the year before he first played officially on the US Tour at Baltusrol. Aoki and Jack Nicklaus were tied on a new 54-hole record score of 207 for the US Open. It was desperately close on the final day which developed into match-play. Aoki had his only three-putt of the championship at the second to let Nicklaus edge ahead and by the turn the Golden Bear had moved two clear. He would never relinquish his lead on a tense afternoon when golf of the very highest calibre was played by both men. Nicklaus still led by two playing the 17th where Aoki hit his second to five feet. Nicklaus was 20 feet away and, typical of the man, holed it. Untypically he ran round the green with a huge grin on his face.

At the par 5 last Aoki needed an eagle to tie and just missed. He had nearly achieved the ambition of every great player and lost an engrossing battle to the best player around. That may have been some consolation. Both he and Nicklaus beat the previous low 72-hole record and collected an additional bonus of $50,000!

Aoki, now 46 with a 21-year-old

daughter, may also be remembered for one, never to be forgotten, shot he hit at Wentworth's second hole – a par 3 over a valley. It was in the 1980 World Match Play when he was defending the title. For him the shot was a 7-iron and he holed it to win not a cheque, or his weight in champagne or a car but a Bovis Group home on a new estate which had just been built at Gleneagles Hotel in Scotland.

Generously he gifted that house for the use of children to enable them to play Gleneagles – a gesture typical of a man whom Gary Player, no less, considers the best in the world from 50 yards from the green. The late Sir Henry Cotton always admired Aoki as a man who plays the game with a most unorthodox style, but a style that made him a very worthy winner of one of Europe's greatest titles – the Panasonic European Championship.

Aoki's short game all week was razor sharp and the first prize cheque he pocketed proved that.

September 1-4, 1983
Old Course, Sunningdale Golf Club, Berkshire.

Prize money; £140,140
Par out: 35, Par in: 35, Yardage: 6,573

								£
1	Isao Aoki	Jap.	65	70	70	69	274	23,330.00
2	Severiano Ballesteros	Spa.	68	75	69	64	276	10,440.00
	Carl Mason	GB	69	73	66	68	276	10,440.00
	Nick Faldo	GB	68	69	68	71	276	10,440.00
5	Greg Norman	Aus.	71	72	68	66	277	5,415.00
	Sam Torrance	GB	68	73	68	68	277	5,415.00
7	Manuel Pinero	Spa.	70	73	70	65	278	3,610.00
	Jose-Maria Canizares	Spa.	70	70	70	68	278	3,610.00
	John Bland	SA	69	67	71	71	278	3,610.00
10	David Frost	SA	67	73	72	68	280	2,700.00
	Michael King	GB	68	68	73	71	280	2,700.00
12	Tony Johnstone	Zim.	70	70	71	70	281	2,380.00
	Denis Durnian	GB	68	71	72	70	281	2,380.00
14	Daivd Jagger	GB	68	72	73	69	282	1,980.00
	Brian Waites	GB	71	73	69	69	282	1,980.00
	Martin Poxon	GB	69	72	70	71	282	1,980.00
	Bernhard Langer	W. Ger.	68	72	71	71	282	1,980.00
	Steve Martin	GB	70	71	69	72	282	1,980.00
19	Gordon Brand, jun.	GB	72	70	74	67	283	1,644.00
	Ewen Murray	GB	66	77	71	69	283	1,644.00
	Harold Henning	SA	67	75	71	70	283	1,644.00
	Ken Brown	GB	72	71	70	70	283	1,644.00
	Jerry Anderson	Can.	71	65	73	74	283	1,644.00

Gordon Richardson of *Golf Illustrated*

The 1984 Panasonic European Open came not long after Severiano Ballesteros' victory in the Open at St Andrews - a win that captured the hearts of all who follow golf. He was favourite to take the title at Sunningdale but in the end came up three shots off the pace, three behind a golfer who had been winless for over a year and a half. While Seve had to accept disappointment yet again and ponder whether the European Open was perhaps his jinx event, Gordon Brand junior, with a red-hot putter, grabbed the first-prize cheque and prevented Seve landing an extra special bonus. Gordon Richardson, writing this time in *Golf Weekly*, wrapped up the proceedings this way:

Gordon Brand junior's second big win of the summer in the Panasonic European Open at Sunningdale completed one of golf's spectacular comebacks - and killed Severiano Ballesteros' hopes of a £75,000 pay-day.

All eyes were on Ballesteros and Howard Clark, who were locked in the lead on seven under par after three rounds. But it was 1982 Rookie of the Year, Brand, who snatched a smash-and-grab win, roaring from three behind to finish three ahead with an outward 29 for a 64 and a 10-under-par total. Perhaps the lack of leader-boards contributed to the downfall of Ballesteros who slipped to a 70 and joint 2nd place with Australian Noel Ratcliffe (65). The Spanish star concentrated on winning his cliff-hanging private duel with Clark, two birdies in the first three holes sweeping him clear of the Yorkshireman. Seve could not hide his astonishment when he reached the first leader-board on the course at the 10th to discover that, instead of being out in front, he was two behind Brand.

From that moment on, he faced an uphill struggle to take the top prize of £25,000 and a bonus of £50,000 offered by Birchgrey for doing the Open and European Open double. Ballesteros, who had looked relaxed and in cool command, went on the attack, but Brand, two holes ahead of him, gave him not an inch. Both men birdied the long 14th, but Seve must have known his chance had gone, barring a Brand blunder, when he chipped too strong to bogey the short 15th. When Brand tangled with two bunkers at the last, Seve needed two birdies to tie, but a woeful pitch and three putts cost him a shot at the 17th.

So Ballesteros, who seeks victories in the European, Portuguese and Italian championships to complete a full set of all eleven European titles, had to settle for joint second prize of £13,025 - but let nothing be taken away from Brand's magnificent victory. He went into action three adrift, but a thunderous opening barrage of eagle-birdie-birdie-par-birdie - five successive threes - rocketed him nine below par. He putted the glassy Sunningdale greens superbly.

He holed from 18 feet and 20 feet on the first two greens, then potted a 25-yard bunker shot at the 5th. Yet, when he bogeyed the next, Ballesteros was a shot ahead again. But a birdie at

George Konig

Over 1500 spectators have a grandstand view at Sunningdale's last hole as Richard Boxall (left, putting), Hugh Baiocchi and eventual winner Gordon Brand, jun, (kneeling) complete their rounds.

the 8th from 12 feet and a birdie three at the 9th for the first 29 of his career put Brand, resplendent in a fluorescent white cap, back in the driving seat and he was never dislodged. His 64 contained only 25 putts and he explained: "I concentrated on decelerating into the ball to get a better run on the putts. I slightly altered my swing - I was taking it back too much on the inside - but the key was my excellent putting.

"It's great to double my winnings to £50,000. After my two wins in 1982, I expected things to happen in 1983. I became complacent and thought the game was a doddle. Now I know I have to work at it. Winning in Galway earlier this year, after twenty months without a win, restored my self-belief. People pointed out that a lot of top players weren't there. They were all at Sunningdale and I still won."

Ratcliffe's brilliant 65 for 2nd place with Ballesteros contained eagles at both par fives and five birdies - the £13,000 prize was double his total winnings for the first five months of the season. Clark had high hopes of stretching an uncanny run of firsts following seconds. Wayne Grady won the German Open the week after finishing runner-up in the Benson and Hedges and Jerry Anderson won the European Masters the week after finishing 2nd in Germany. Clark,

Seventh European Open

stroke edge over Clark and Ballesteros ran into trouble at the dog-leg 11th. He ended in a ditch to the right of the fairway and, after a lengthy deliberation with partners Gary Player and Jerry Anderson, he deemed it a lateral water hazard and dropped away, ending with a triple-bogey seven.

After Nick had signed his card and left the course, a Sunningdale member informed PGA officials that the ditch was a water hazard. Faldo had breached the rules by not keeping the hazard between him and the hole when dropping, and tournament director Tony Gray had no option but to disqualify him.

So another European Open had provided no shortage of personal drama, human disappointment and glorious triumph over a course which seemed somehow to reflect the stylish way the tournament was being staged each season. Just four years after it had been saved from extinction the European Open was well en route to a treasured spot on the golfing calendar.

There were no prizes for guessing what retired Sunningdale professional Arthur Lees and Gary Player talked about when they met during the week. In May 1956 the 20-year-old Player announced his arrival in big-time golf by pipping Arthur, then 48, by two strokes in the Dunlop 90-hole tournament at the club. This time Gary did not land the first prize but the crowds were pleased to see him back and he enjoyed playing Sunningdale again.

South African Jeff Hawkes (top) equalled the course record of 63 on the second day but Howard Clark (above) failed to maintain a winning sequence started by Wayne Grady in Germany and continued by Jerry Anderson at Crans.

runner-up in Switzerland, failed to continue the trend. His hopes foundered on a shaky start, but a brave birdie at the last squeezed him into joint 4th place with Richard Boxall, a 21 year old from Camberley, who had to pre-qualify. Richard fired a closing 67 to win £6,900 and triple his earnings for the year. A dramatic three-shot swing over the last two holes hauled Ballesteros level with Clark with a round to go. Seve coaxed in a 25-footer to birdie the 18th and Clark bogeyed the 17th and 18th.

South African Jeff Hawkes set the sparks flying on day two with a 63 that equalled Manuel Pinero's course record. His round included three eagles, two penalty strokes and a missed 10 inch putt. Hawkes, who got into the event via a pre-qualifying play-off, had to be content with joint 2nd with Brand, two behind Clark, at the half-way stage. But the second day's biggest headlines, however, were reserved for Nick Faldo's shock disqualification after slipping to a 73 for 138. Faldo, whose opening 65 had given him a one-

Gary Player got out of any trouble he was in easily enough. His playing partner Nick Faldo was less fortunate on the second day.

Brand, jun.

Renton Laidlaw of *The Evening Standard*

There is a built-in modesty about the 1984 winner of the European Open at Sunningdale. Ask Gordon Brand junior about his golf game and he will answer unprepossessingly that he is an average to long driver, a "not bad" iron player and can from time to time be quite reasonable on the greens. In fact he underestimates his talent. He can, on any one week, prove unbeatable and has on no fewer than six occasions since joining the professionals in 1981, rather earlier than he had planned after being left out of the Walker Cup team that played the Americans at Shinnecock Hills that year . . . but more of that in a moment.

Gordon is referred to often enough as the son of the Scottish professional at Knowle in Bristol. His father has the same name. Gordon uses junior after his name as a result but that also helps to differentiate between him and another Gordon Brand on the European Tour – the one from Yorkshire. They are constantly being confused with each other and neither really cares any more. Neither has an identity crisis. Both know where they are going even if Brand junior does not set himself goals like Gary Player to keep himself on course for bigger title wins. He is rather too laid-back for that . . . but do not confuse his apparent *laissez-faire* attitude for a lack of determination. Gordon is no advocate of *que sera, sera*. He sometimes does make things happen. He is a battler when he wants to be and has always had that inborn self-belief so important to any champion.

As son of a professional you might think he was playing golf, like Scottish Ryder Cup colleague and former European Open winner Sandy Lyle, from a tender age. Sandy had a club in his hands at the age of three. Well, you would be wrong. Gordon did not take up golf until he was ten and was not hooked until he was at least fourteen. You see his father was not a professional initially. He was a good, solid, reliable Gloucestershire County player who was asked to become pro at Knowle when Tom MacNaughton left for Australia when Gordon junior was ten. Father Brand, who was a carpenter by trade,

Gordon Brand, jun., seems to produce his best on tight tree-lined courses. He certainly did round Sunningdale in 1984 and his win proved his Galway success was no fluke.

jumped at the challenge and junior was established in a golfing environment.

He had caddied from time to time for his father but he was not immediately hooked when he found himself in a position to play and practise every day. For four years he was unmoved by the game in which he has become a star. He was quietly encouraged but left to make up his own mind. He was fourteen when he decided that there could be something in golf for him and that if he stuck in, lowered his 25-handicap and made the club team, he might be able to leave school and make a living playing the game.

"I was not a good pupil at school. Indeed my mother was despondent at my progress and worried about what I might end up doing," says Gordon. She and his father must have been delighted that eventually he caught the bug and made progress quickly enough to be playing off scratch three years later after having decided there was something enjoyable and challenging about knocking a small, white, dimpled ball around. By the time he was 17 he knew he had made up his mind to turn professional but there was a great deal he had to do in amateur golf first. He had an apprenticeship to serve. He had to learn how to cope better with the pressure that is exerted when you play yourself into a winning position. In some respects getting into contention is the easier part. Staying there and then going on to win is what separates the men from the boys. From early on in his national amateur career Gordon Brand, jun., showed he had those extra qualities.

Gordon travelled regularly the 400 miles north each year to play in the Scottish equivalent of the English tournaments in which Sandy Lyle and Ken Brown, another Ryder Cup Scot based in England were competing. "I remember," he says, "going to the Scottish Boys' Championship over the West Links at North Berwick one year and at Dunbar another. I never seemed to do all that well for some reason and remember that having been knocked out in the third round I found myself trudging to the station in a snowstorm – and that was in April. I remember pulling the big black mackintosh around me. It was cold – far colder than it ever seemed to be in Bristol where we stayed."

Brand had made it his job once he had decided he liked the game and had an aptitude for it to get into the Knowle Club's Stragglers team – a side for children between eight and sixteen who showed talent. Then he was in the second team, the full club side and played county golf. Before he had left school he had been a dedicated practiser. He would go out and hit shots in the early morning before anyone was up at the club, would practise pitch and putt whenever he had a free moment and, after helping his father take in the flags at night, he would again head for the practice ground. "I was not happy if I was not hitting balls or practising," he says. "Golf was my life and I sacrificed everything for it at that time and thank goodness I did."

He had won a couple of 36-hole tournaments in the region when he made his first big breakthrough. It came in 1978 at

that most picturesque of championship courses – Woodhall Spa owned privately by Neil Hotchkin. It is a delightful spot in deepest Lincolnshire and still one of Brand's favourite courses. It is tree lined and demands accuracy off the tee. Brand had that all right, so much so that when they held the British Youths there a year later he won again and never lost a match in the Britain and Ireland match against the Continent and the England-Scotland competition that preceded the event. Accuracy and steadiness was the cornerstone of his game. At Woodhall Spa he could shape shots. Winning did not demand massive power off the tee. It is not a slogger's course, it is one that demands finesse. He had it and proved that, once he had a chance of winning, he took it.

He is not easily frightened of people and was not that week or the weeks in Scotland when he won the Scottish Stroke-play Championship at Monktonhall and the Scottish Youths at Monifieth in 1980. By the end of 1980 he had played in a Walker Cup match, two St Andrews Trophy matches – that is Great Britain and Ireland against the Continent of Europe – had competed for Britain in the Eisenhower Trophy, the World Amateur Team Championship and was, of course, a Scottish international.

He won abroad, too, in Portugal and Sweden, doing better in strokes-play events than in match-play. His record shows that, and the selectors were only too well aware of it as well. He sums it up himself as "abysmal" but even so he was in for a rude shock in 1981. He had remained amateur for that year, planning to play in one more Walker Cup before turning pro. The problem was he did not make the team. He was dropped by the selectors who reckoned his head/head play was far inferior to his card-and-pencil form. The fact was that he was a steady player who hit few bad shots. His consistency paid off in stroke-play, but lesser players willing to take chances in the knowledge that, at worst, it would mean only the loss of one hole, would beat him. In fact he dreaded match-play at that time. He did not enjoy it

David Cannon

Gordon Brand, jun., was in two bunkers at the last but made very few mistakes over the four days of the championship and was just too good for title-chasing Seve.

but was still surprised when, having been in the four-man Eisenhower Trophy side months before, he was dropped for the twelve-man Walker Cup team. That precipitated his move to the professional ranks and, in the long run, did no harm at all.

"He played in pro-ams in the South-West region, received an invitation to play in the Scottish Championship at Dalmahoy, rather poorly as it turned out," but his snub by the selectors proved a blessing in disguise. He had had no money. The money he won in the pro-ams meant that by the time he went off to Portugal to earn his Tour ticket at the school he had £3–£4,000 in his pocket, was not worried about having to find a sponsor and his relaxed attitude was underlined when he won the school.

That winter to gain more experience he headed off to the Sunshine circuit in South Africa and, in his second tournament came joint-2nd to Gary Player in the Lexington PGA Championship at The Wanderers. Open Champion Bill Rogers tied him that year and Mark McNulty, who would go on to become a multiple champion, was just in behind. It all seemed so easy. He never missed a half-way cut and returned to England showing a profit of well over £4,000

and was set to play his first season on the European Tour. What an impact he made. He was easily Rookie of the Year and winner of the late Sir Henry Cotton's prize. No rookie had ever finished with over £40,000 in one season nor as high as 7th. Of course it helped that he won two events that first year which had started so well for him in Tunisia, at El Kantouai where he came 3rd to Manuel Calero of Spain. His first pro win was at Porthcawl where he won the Coral's Welsh Classic and later that year he took the Bob Hope Classic.

"In those days before the all-exempt Tour, it was important to finish in the top 60 at the end of each season," says Brand. "People told me if I did that and kept my card I was doing well but that first year out only six players finished ahead of me. It was great and I paid the penalty for easing off my schedule and not working as hard during the following winter as I should have."

In fact, considered a certainty for the Ryder Cup in 1983, Gordon missed out. His close season complacency saw him drop back to 34th in the money list. Since then he has never relaxed as much again during the winter. In fact he admits: "If I have gone a couple of weeks without practising I get very edgy. I keep thinking that when I pick up the clubs again I am going to play like a 24-handicapper. I never believe it is going to be there again. I worry that I may have lost the feel of the club."

Not that he believes he was born with a feel for the game. He thinks the hours and hours spent on the practice ground are what really matter. It is there you learn so much. It is there you teach the hands how to work the ball. It is a grind but that is golf and all the top players are hard workers. There is no substitute for hard work on the range according to Brand, who came back in 1984 to win twice in Galway and then at Sunningdale in the Panasonic European Open. With amateur Alan Lyddon he had won the Sunningdale Foursomes, so had a rapport with the famous course. Like Woodhall Spa, Sunningdale is tree lined and he always feels very much at home there. He certainly did in the last round when he shot a 64 and pulverised the field.

If Gordon recalled how he had felt all the strength draining from him after he won his first event in Wales two years earlier it was all so different now. The adrenalin was flowing as he raced away to a victory that earned him a place in the World series at Akron, Ohio (where he finished 7th) and also guaranteed him a spot, too, in Scotland's World Cup team. He and Sam Torrance came second to the Spaniards in Rome.

Brand recalls how he started that great final round at Sunningdale – 3, 3, 3, 3, 3 – an eagle and three birdies in that opening stretch. The round was made there and he never let it slip, but then he is not easily intimidated, not easily put off by the reputations of his rivals. He has, like everyone, tremendous admiration for Severiano Ballesteros, and is always very conscious when the Spaniard is on the leader-board with him, but he concentrates always on playing the course, refusing to be drawn into the trap of going out to try and beat one person such as Seve. There are so many potential winners on tour that it would be daft to worry about one man and end up losing to someone else having a good day.

"We all know if Seve is playing at his best it is going to be tough for us to win, but you can only go out and do your best," says Brand who comes into that category of European golfer who fails to get the invitations which would allow him to play regularly in America. It does not worry him too much. He has, in fact, turned down US invitations because he is happy playing in Europe where the money now is so good. Does this show a lack of ambition on his part or a sensible approach? The fact is that he does not want to become a Trans-Atlantic jet-setter like the others.

That is not for him. . . not at the moment anyway. Maybe later, but he and wife Sheena, heavily involved in equestrianism and seldom seen on the golf Tour, prefer things just the way they are – and no one could ever doubt Gordon knows what he wants from life and golf. . .

One of the most exciting moments of his career was making the Ryder Cup and playing in that history-making side that beat the Americans on their home ground for the first time. "It was marvellous from the moment I stepped on to Concorde for the first time to fly to America. What impressed me most was the dedication shown by Seve

Almost there! Gordon Brand, jun. waits anxiously by the last green for arch rival Seve Ballesteros to complete his round. A minute later the tension was lifted as Brand was confirmed Panasonic European Open Champion.

and Sandy and Nick and Bernhard. They all wanted to win so much. The desire was in their eyes and it rubbed off on the whole team. He was not played the first morning but in the afternoon fourballs was teamed up with Jose Rivero and beat Ben Crenshaw and the reigning US Open Champion Scott Simpson in the top match! "I remember being so nervous on the first tee. I could be leading a major event with a round to go and not feel so nervous. You were very aware that at Muirfield Village it was not for you but for your country," says the patriotic Brand who lost a foursomes with Rivero and fourball with Eamonn Darcy the next day and halved on the last day in the singles against Hal Sutton. Significantly Jacklin had put him out in what might have been the most crucial spot of all in the line-up – last.

These days he is easily recognisable on the course with his white cap. He has had many since he first wore one at the European Open at Sunningdale. Now none of his contracts are signed without the sponsor querying where his advertising can go on the cap. Last year he had Slazenger on the front; this year, having changed clubs, he has Mizuno on the back.

He is very much a professional's professional. Not a loner in the strictest sense of the word, but a player who keeps himself to himself. He does not hang around the clubhouses. You will not find him in the bar too often. He does his job and leaves. The golf course is his office. When he has done his job he goes home or to the hotel. It is a frustrating life travelling the circuit but Gordon Brand, jun., has the temperament to cope with the delays. There is, he says, nothing you can do about it but be patient, stay cool, accept it just as those people who commute day in and day out to London accept the inconvenience and aggravation of it all.

He can, he admits, become moody and irritable if he is not playing well. If the putts are not dropping or his iron-play is not as sharp as it should be or his driving is off he finds it all so tiresome. He does not set himself goals for fear of disappointments. For him happiness on the circuit is playing well and if he wins along the way from time to time that is fine. The fact is that by working hard and putting considerable effort into the game he does play well enough to win, especially when it matters. Needing two victories to make the last Ryder Cup team automatically, he went out and, in successive weeks, won in Holland and Sweden to clinch his place. That was typical of a young man who may not realise the potential he has, or may be quite happy not to – for the moment. He will be around for a long, long time. Gordon Brand, jun., knows exactly how to organise his golfing life. It may be less international than some of his colleagues but maybe they envy him more than he does them.

September 6-9, 1984
Old Course, Sunningdale Golf Club, Berkshire.

Prize money; £151,144
Par out: 35, Par in: 35, Yardage: 6,573

								£
1	Gordon Brand, jun.	GB	67	66	73	64	270	25,000.00
2	Noel Ratcliffe	Aus.	67	74	67	65	273	13,025,00
	Severiano Ballesteros	Spa.	66	68	69	70	273	13,025.00
4	Richard Boxall	GB	71	69	67	67	274	6,930.00
	Howard Clark	GB	66	65	72	71	274	6,930.00
6	Lanny Wadkins	USA	69	67	70	70	276	5,250.00
7	Keith Waters	GB	72	69	68	68	277	4,125.00
	Bernard Gallacher	GB	68	69	68	72	277	4,125.00
9	Bob Charles	NZ	73	67	70	68	278	3,182.50
	Manuel Pinero	Spa.	69	69	71	69	278	3,182.50
11	Eamonn Darcy	Ire.	71	70	72	66	279	2,498.00
	Bill McColl	GB	72	71	68	68	279	2,498.00
	Craig DeFoy	GB	74	69	68	68	279	2,498.00
	Tony Johnstone	Zim.	73	67	68	71	279	2,498.00
	Sam Torrance	GB	73	70	65	71	279	2,498.00
16	Tommy Horton	GB	70	70	68	72	280	2,090.00
	Vicente Fernandez	Arg.	67	68	73	72	280	2,090.00
18	Warren Humphreys	GB	73	64	75	69	281	1,731.25
	Ian Mosey	GB	71	70	70	70	281	1,731.25
	Ove Sellberg	Swe.	69	74	68	70	281	1,731.25
	Christy O'Connor, jun.	Ire.	69	71	69	72	281	1,731.25
	Stephen Bennett	GB	71	71	66	73	281	1,731.25
	Eddie Polland	GB	72	71	65	73	281	1,731.25
	Manuel Calero	Spa.	69	69	67	76	281	1,731.25

Mark Wilson

Above, the famous clubhouse in 1903, and below, Bobby Jones, Gold Vase winner of 1930, being congratulated by Diana Fishwick, British Ladies Open Champion.

The many enviable qualities that today cause Panasonic European Open Championship venue Sunningdale to be respected throughout the golf world are plain for all to see and appreciate. But it was not always so. The heathland waste above a remote railway station sited by accident on the then unfashionable side of the village, offered a far from inviting picture when Tom "T.A." Roberts and his brother George came upon the scene late in the last century. Fortunately, they were avid golfers in search of a new home, relatively wealthy, full of the Victorian spirit for pioneering and empire building, and sharing a form of double vision to be enjoyed. The barren and windswept area at the crest of the hill, served only by a bridle path, would be perfect, they decided, not only for the construction of a fine house to be called Ridgemount, but also the development of an inland golf course worthy of comparison with the great seaside links.

The gift of hindsight now makes it easy to see that Sunningdale was destined to become famous for sport and a home for competitiveness of the highest order. There are those who might argue King Henry VIII set the scene, though in questionable fashion, when the whole area was a part of Windsor Forest in which he regularly hunted.

The future of Sunningdale as a place for golf was more directly influenced by Henry suppressing the Benedictine Nunnery of Broomhall so that its land comprising the Sunningdale Estate in 1524 passed to St John's College, Cambridge. It was to St John's, 374 years later, that Tom and George Roberts, armed with tremendous foresight, successfully pleaded for leaseholds allowing the building of the golf course and houses of "appropriate high quality" in the neighbourhood.

While completing their own home in 1898 (much later it was to be greatly enlarged and became the Dormy House on Ridgemount Hill), they began the complex business of establishing Sunningdale Golf Club. Friends were recruited to form a Founders' Committee, and Willie Park, son of the first Open Champion, was given £3,800 with orders to design and create a course of exemplary character. He did as instructed, though what he produced as a classic test for the gutty ball has been greatly changed in the years since to keep pace with the development of golf.

The need for a clubhouse was met with eight builders being invited to tender for the work at a maximum cost of £6,000. The sombrely written minutes of the committee meeting on 19 July 1900, cannot disguise the shock of opening the envelopes and finding the lowest bid to be £7,699. In readiness for the grand opening of the course in 1901, Jack White became the club's first professional –"his remuneration not to exceed £1 a week and a cottage on the links." Matters improved considerably when he won the Open Championship three years later: it was agreed to join his cottage to the water supply! Hugh Maclean was recruited as head greenkeeper on a trial basis of three months for 36 shillings a week and cottage, or 40 shillings without shelter. He eventually retired in 1939. The post of secretary at an annual salary of £150 attracted 435 applications, and Harry S. Colt was successful. It was to prove a learning experience in many ways.

Throughout this formative process, strong emphasis was placed on the fact that Sunningdale was intended as a "club for gentlemen". It was 1948 before ladies were admitted as associate members. In the meantime they were treated to such extremes of chauvinistic attitudes that the committee at one stage hastened to insure the premises for £1,000 against retribution by suffragettes. Small wonder when for years a notice in the smoking room unashamedly proclaimed that women could only attend the club on sufferance. Concessions came slowly, beginning with a change of rules that allowed them to be invited to the club for tea, providing they came after four o'clock and stayed in the hall.

Momentous events in the history of the club often amount to a few words in the red leather-bound minute books Colt maintained in pristine condition. The first charge to visitors on the course is fixed at one shilling a round providing they play with a member. Lord Stanley's plea for ladies to be allowed to play the course at weekends was, however, refused. Soon after there was a change of heart: the committee agreed that they could play on

David Cannon

Sundays - after 3.15 p.m. and in mixed foursomes. For them, 1903 became a year to remember.

It would be irresponsible of any writer or historian to overlook the fact that over the years one or two of the members, and, indeed, the odd professional, has been known to indulge in a modest wager. The first officially recorded instance is dated 15 April 1905, when the committee acknowledged the receipt of a letter from the local vicar, the Reverend J. Cornish, who complained of caddies being worked on Sundays, and betting on the club premises. The secretary was instructed to write and assure the Reverend that every possible precaution was taken to prevent the employment of small boys on Sundays before 1 p.m. As to gambling at Sunningdale, nothing was known.

After the First World War Sunningdale resumed life with strengthened ambitions to flourish at an even faster pace than before. It was an urge answered by the building in the early 1920s of a second course, the New, designed by H.S. Colt who had progressed from

secretary to golf architect of considerable renown. Subsequent tinkering with both the Old and New courses has resulted in the world-wide recognition of Sunningdale's 36 holes as a golfing masterpiece. It remains, nevertheless, an intriguing exercise to visualise the hallowed Old course as it was originally laid out by Park to meet the challenge of the gutty ball at the turn of the century.

Until its development by the Ridgemount Estate Company, and the pioneering of Britain's first purpose-built golf community, the Sunningdale property consisted of three farms: Broomhall, Titlarks and Stavehall. The rest was a vast expanse of heather, gorse, some pine trees and the odd oak, the most splendid example of all being the veteran that still towers beside the clubhouse. It is, of course, the source of the club's emblem so well known to the world.

Before Colt laid out the New course in 1922, and there have been a number of major changes since to give it a stature second only to its elder brother, the Old, another nine holes

The beauty of Sunningdale today - the 5th and 6th holes from the 5th tee.

Sunningdale

HRH The Prince of Wales KG, the Captain of the Club in 1930.

Red Cross Day, 1917. The club raised £1,500 in the auction sale - at present day rates a fantastic sum.

had been developed on what is now the practice ground, and the Titlarks Hill area. It was often referred to as the "Chauffeur Course".

While the emphasis will always be on maintaining the club for the benefit of its members, both the Old and New courses are frequently made available to important tournaments for the encouragement of the game generally, and that includes the Panasonic European Open. The first of these occasions was in 1903 when the Old was the stage for the very first professional match-play championship sponsored by the *News of the World.* Many more major professional and amateur events for men, women and juniors have followed. Fittingly, the hosting of the 1987 Walker Cup matches, the first to be played on an inland course in Britain, is the latest of Sunningdale's pioneeering ventures in the spirit intended by the Roberts brothers. The same spirit has fortified the annual staging since 1934 of the immensely popular Sunningdale foursomes, unique in allowing any combination of amateur or professsional, man or woman. Its success has now become something of an embarrassment with the entry list always being grossly over-subscribed.

It is possible only to touch upon most aspects of the Sunningdale history; a whole book could be written on the remakable characters who served so long and loyally as club servants. One of these was James Sheridan, a fearlessly outspoken Scot who arrived on a six weeks' trial as caddiemaster and was still there nearly 60 years later waiting for the job to be made permanent. Sheridan became a Sunningdale legend perpetuated by his own book, *Sheridan of Sunningdale,* which will probably never be bettered as a history of the club that made him an honorary member and placed his portrait in oils on the clubhouse wall after it had first been hung at the Royal Academy.

During his 56 years as caddiemaster awaiting confirmation of being appointed, Sheridan developed an authority that could withstand the wrath of any member. Anyone giving a caddie less than fair treatment was guaranteed the sharp edge of Sheridan's tongue. He never minced his words, not even to the Prince of Wales and his brother the Duke of York when they were captains of Sunningdale. The Prince, to become the uncrowned King, was in the habit of changing his shoes in Sheridan's office on arriving at the club. "Which course am I using today?" he asked one day when his golf was going through a period of struggle. "The New course," came the answer. "Dammit, Sheridan, you know I prefer the Old course," complained the Prince. "Ay, sir, but the New course is wider," insisted the fearless caddiemaster, and there was no further argument. Hugh MacLean and his son Jimmy successively held the post of greenkeeper for the first 73 years of Sunningdale's existence. Bert Chapman, as a boy, worked in the village greengrocery until he was instantly sacked for taking a Saturday afternoon off to watch the Cup Final. Then he heard about a "golf course being built up the hill" and he went to MacLean to ask for work. "Can you dig?" asked MacLean. "I can do anything," said Chapman. Sixty glorious years later he was still serving Sunningdale Golf Club, doing anything that needed to be done.

Another loyal servant was Arthur Wigmore, holder of the Distinguished Conduct Medal, who ran, in every sense, the locker rooms for 50 years. He too, had his own way with Royalty. One day he came upon the Duke of York wandering round the clubhouse and appearing troubled. "If you are looking for your brother he's in the dining room," was Wigmore's unsolicited advice. A proven case of mixing with kings and still retaining the common touch.

Long service has also been a strength of the professional's shop. It has had only seven tenants – Jack White, who employed six clubmakers at one time, Ernest Sales, Michael Bingham, Percy Boomer, Arthur Lees, who retired after 26 years but remains a sought-after teacher, Clive Clark, and, at present, Keith Maxwell. The club secretaries, from Harry Colt through to Keith Almond today, make an equally impressive list – including the one who was so upset on seeing a lady wearing slacks that he immediately posted a notice that declared: "Women playing golf in trousers must take them off before entering the clubhouse."

As the fortunes of ladies have improved so have the two golf courses with the help of

Photographs Courtesy of Sunningdale Golf Club

Looking down on the 12th Green during the 1938 Foursomes Competition.

celebrated architects, including Ken Cotton and, more lately, Donald Steel. By modern standards the Old - the European Open course - remains rather short, but what it may lack in length it certainly makes amends for in subtlety. The most celebrated round in Sunningdales's history however, was played in 1926 when the immortal Bobby Jones qualified for the Open Championship, which he was to win. One of his qualifying rounds was a score of 66 on the Old course. It was close to perfection: 33 shots, 33 putts with hickory shafts and an inferior ball. The world acclaimed it - but the Sunningdale committee of the day proved difficult to please. Members urged that the feat should be marked with a plaque. The committee refused, declaring, "It does not seem appropriate to commemorate by a permanent tablet in the clubhouse what after all is only an isolated instance of good scoring." Happily, a copy of his score card hangs today in the clubhouse.

The Suggestions Book, as with all golf clubs, offers a fascinating study of changing times. Sunningdale adopted a proposal to have one in 1906, and the second entry - following a contentious call to move the 13th tee back behind the hill - put priorities in order for many of the members. The charge of one shilling and twopence for a whisky and Schweppes should be reduced to tenpence, it was urged. The committee answered with a compromise. They cut the price to exactly one shilling, but it was the opening of the floodgates. In no time at all the book contained a suggestion that two shillings for lunch was excessive. Again the committee yielded.

Progress since Tom and George Roberts chanced upon Sunningdale's heathland with golf in mind has suffered the odd stumble, but thanks to a succession of members, notably the late Gerald Micklem CBE, whose overriding passion was always to further the best interests of the game and the club, a long road has been travelled. Or should it be bridle path? It has needed dedication, determination, ingenuity, and, always, a large measure of optimism. The ingenuity exampled by the founder brothers, and the kind of eternal optimism one of Sheridan's caddies displayed the morning he went to the tee to surprise his regular employer by being completely sober. "Good gracious, you haven't had a drink," said the bewildered member. "No sir, but it's early yet, and I am very hopeful," answered the caddie. Sunningdale Golf Club is equally hopeful, on a much higher plane, with its ambitions to continue to command world esteem and, in this respect, The Panasonic European Open, helps further the clubs reputation.

Gordon Richardson of *Golf Illustrated*

David Cannon

Bernhard Langer, with victory well within his grasp, could afford to have a bit of fun with a local "copper" as he walked up the last hole.

Bernhard Langer won his first and, to date, only major – the US Masters – in 1985 when he held off Severiano Ballesteros' challenge on the back stretch at Augusta. Seve did not push him too hard, however, in the 1985 Panasonic European Open and neither did reigning Open Champion Sandy Lyle, Ian Woosnam or Nick Faldo, but then as Gordon Richardson explained in *Golf Illustrated*, Langer was at the height of his playing power. He could do little wrong.

Behind the scenes, too, there was plenty happening as Alan Booth of *Golf Illustrated* discovered, but it was Bernhard Langer who scooped the big prize, the headlines and the helmet!

Not for nothing is Bernhard Langer labelled "The Munich Money Machine". He followed up his

fifteen below par German Open triumph seven days earlier with an eleven under par Panasonic European Open victory at Sunningdale to nudge his prize winnings this year to a stunning £389,617. In nine outings in Europe he has picked up £115,716 – or £12,857.30 a week. Yet Langer confirmed, after the famous Red Devils parachuted out of the clouds with his £33,320 cheque, that he is handing the top European money winner tag to Open Champion Sandy Lyle. He would bypass the Ebel European Masters (last of the jackpot open events) in favour of an exhibition in Paris involving Mark O'Meara and Billy Casper, and compete only in the Suntory World Match Play Championship and the Ryder Cup. His remaining diary dates concern contests in Japan, Australia and Hawaii.

Langer, whose other 1985 victories

came in the US and Australian Masters and the Heritage Classic, followed rounds of 61, 60, 62 at the shortened flooded course in Bremen with 66, 72, 64, 67 at Sunningdale, a total of 269 leaving him three strokes clear of nearest challenger John O'Leary. Then he quietly announced to the assembled press that his ambition was "to improve"! He explained: "I'm not driving the ball as far as I used to. In May I switched drivers to gain more accuracy and lost 10 or 12 yards. But I'm not hitting it any straighter so I might as well go back to a club that gives me more length. I've been sent three or four nice heads by Wilsons. Now I'm looking for a shaft that gives me the right trajectory. It's been a very satisfactory year. I've had seasons when I've won more but I've never been more consistent. In nine tournaments in Europe I've only finished out of the top ten once. But I still feel my best years are to come. You learn something every time you are under pressure. My aim is to continue to improve and to win more tournaments."

Langer, so relaxed he donned a policeman's helmet as he strode through the throng ringing the 18th green, was always in the driving seat after defending Champion Gordon Brand junior, with whom he shared the overnight lead at eight under par, and Spain's Jose-Maria Canizares, who started seven under, slipped away, Brand dropping three shots in the first six holes and Canizares three in two holes from the turn.

Surprisingly it was O'Leary who started the week in 43rd place in the Epson Order of Merit, who emerged as his chief challenger. Severiano Ballesteros never quite got his act together, having to settle for a 68 and a five below par 275, which left him sharing seventh place with Canizares, Japan's Tommy Nakajima, who dropped two shots in the last four holes after eagling the 14th to go seven under, and Bernard Gallacher.

Greg Norman, the half-way leader, ended on a disappointing 278 after a 72, and Lyle, who slumped to a 74, ended a miserable one over par on 281 with Nick Faldo, who, after all his troubles, played a little more solidly but could not manage a single birdie in a closing 73. Ian Woosnam, as he had done at the Benson and

Gordon Brand jun., the winner in 1984, got caught up too often in the heather a year later.

David Cannon

Eighth European Open

Hedges earlier in the summer, flashed through the field to set the last day target, this time with a 65 (he had birdied five of the last six on day three for a 67) for a final 274. But that proved good enough only for sixth spot, a stroke behind Brand junior (71), Howard Clark, finishing in high style with a 67, and Des Smyth, who looked set to tie O'Leary but had to take a penalty drop at the last after his drive drifted among the roots of a giant gorse bush. He shot 68.

O'Leary who suffered a back injury after lessons from Bob Torrance sharpened his game got his reward for a season of consistent improvement. Apart from the Open he had played four rounds in every European event in which he had competed. He enjoyed two strokes of good fortune - chipping from the trees and holing from 12 feet for par at the 5th and chipping in from 30 yards to eagle the 14th - to shoot 68 for 272 and earn a career-best £22,000, over £9,000 more than he got for winning the 1982 Carrolls Irish Open. It set up even more riches, lifting him into the Irish top three for the £1 million Dunhill Cup at St Andrews. It was quite a day for the Irish for

Craig DeFoy missed the half-way cut and announced he would be retiring from the full-time tournament scene.

Smyth, with his £10,333 prize, also overtook non-qualifier Eamonn Darcy to join Christy O'Connor junior in the team.

Yet nothing should detract from Langer's winning performance - one of quality, determination and style. Yet again the Panasonic European Open had produced a classy winner. Yet again it had taken an outstanding performance to win the prestige title at an event which was now attracting world interest.

For two Euro Tour players, who have been on the circuit since the mid-60s, the Panasonic European Open virtually marked the end of their tournament careers. Both are now in club jobs in Surrey - 36-year-old Nick Job at the Richmond Club at Sudbrook and Craig DeFoy, 38, at Coombe Hill.

Job found unexpected form on the first day at Sunningdale, with a four under par 66, but DeFoy slumped to 78 and as he missed the half-way cut the next day said, "That could be my last tournament." Before arriving at Sunningdale, Job had won only £949 in six outings that season and Defoy was little better with £1,295 from seven events. For both, their chances of staying in the top 125 of the Epson Order of Merit at the end of the season were remote. Job had been appointed a club pro that April and said, "I'm enjoying it - and with a family (his wife Penny and two children aged four and one) it is time to establish a sound future, and I

Nick Faldo, in a spot of bother here, had more problems than usual. His regular caddie retired the week before the championship.

don't think I can do it in tournament golf. I have played every year since 1967 and this is probably the last."

DeFoy, with a wife and three children some years older than Job's, has been on the tour for twenty years, and was a World Cup player for Wales on seven occasions. He won five tournaments in Zambia and was runner-up in the Match Play Championship in 1976. Job also won in East Africa in the Victoria Falls Classic the same year, and two years later tied for first place in the Greater Manchester Open, losing in the play-off. Both Job and DeFoy made headlines in the Open Championship. DeFoy's final rounds of 70, 69 at Royal Birkdale in 1971 left him in fourth place behind Lee Trevino, and Job had rounds of 70, 69 to be only a stroke behind Bill Rogers at the half-way stage at Sandwich in 1981.

The European Open in 1985 also saw Nick Faldo operating with a new caddy after Ulsterman David McNeilly decided to give up. He had been working with Faldo for three years including in America when he won the Heritage Classic at Sea Pines.

After Faldo had missed the cut in the Benson and Hedges International, he asked McNeilly to phone him during the week. But back home, McNeilly wrote to Faldo saying he was quitting - and he is now thinking of finding some other form of activity in golf.

Faldo's first caddie, John Moorhouse, who was a member with Faldo as an amateur at the Welwyn Garden City club, now caddies for Mark James.

When he arrived at Sunningdale, Faldo had some comments to make about the swing change which had resulted in indifferent form this season. "I started to change my swing in May - perhaps it would have been better if I had kept quiet about altering it, then no one would have been concerned and constantly asking me about it," he said. "I have been working at it and I can't go back. I am playing the right way, but it is taking time. It is true I have not been doing well for a while, but you have to persevere with what you are doing and what you know is going to be best for you in the long run."

Andy Podger took over the job and Nick's swing change helped him win the Open.

The Irish contingent did well - notably Des Smyth.

David Cannon

Eighth European Open

David Cannon

Aussie Greg Norman was grateful for the advice of an old master at Sunningdale. After a first round 67, Norman went immediately to the putting green. He had three-putted twice and missed from 10 feet on the last green for a birdie. As he was practising his putting stroke, Sunningdale's veteran Ryder Cup player Arthur Lees, one of golf's all-time favourites, watched Norman and then said, "No, that's no good." Arthur Lees, for so many years the club's professional, pointed out to the Australian that he was moving his arms backwards and forwards, resulting in an erratic stroke. After a few minutes, Norman began to find the right stroke and rhythm, and as Lees left him to continue his practice, he was holing the four and five footers which had been giving him problems during his round but not enough of them to take the title.

The eagle eye of New Zealander Bob Charles caused a stir on the first day. Former Open Champion Charles, in the eleventh match of the day, inspected the line of his putt after reaching the green at the first hole – and then said, "This hole is too small." Charles would not putt out until the hole had been measured – and it was then found the diameter was 4 inches instead of the statutory 4¼ inches. When the hole had been widened to its correct diameter, Charles proceeded to putt out, taking a par 5 to start his round, and continuing with par figures before getting his first birdie at the 9th. He finished with a one under par 69. A year previously, Charles complained about a tee board at the second hole. As a left-hander, he said it impeded his swing – and removed the board, which cost him a two-stroke penalty and a round of 71.

Greg Norman had no problem with his iron-play – but he needed a putting tip from Sunningdale's much respected veteran pro Arthur Lees.

Langer

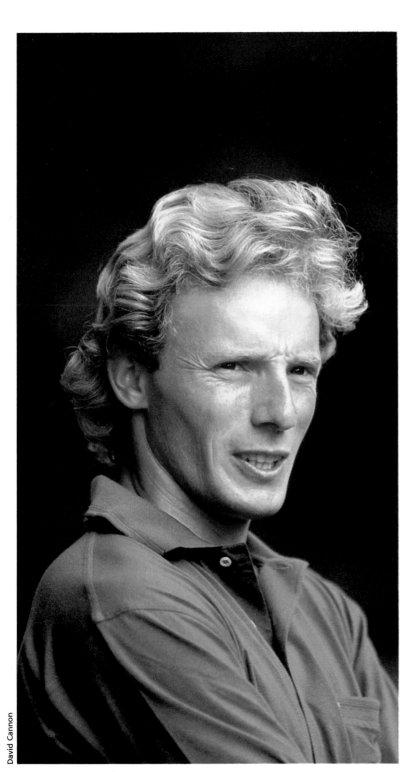

David Cannon

Few, if any, golfers in the history of the game have worked harder or longer to improve their technique and sharpen their talent than West Germany's Bernhard Langer. Sheer, hard, unrelenting graft comes naturally to this man whose own family had to overcome enormous odds just to survive, during and after, the Second World War.

His father, Erwin, was born in Sudetanland, now part of Czechoslovakia but a German territory in 1939. The Langers were farmers and, but for conscription into the German Army, Erwin, too, would have worked on the land for his living. Instead he had to spend six years as a courier, a part of his life that ended in May 1945 when he was captured by the Russians.

After several months in a POW camp Erwin Langer was herded on to a train along with several hundred other prisoners. Their destination was unknown. What was known was that they were to be taken back across what were now Russian lines. It was not a prospect that filled Erwin or his fellow prisoners on the train with any great joy. Rumours of forced labour down mines swept the carriages as the train trundled across Germany and headed for the Czech border. A few miles before the border the train had to slow to climb a steep hill. By now it was night and the guards were tired and careless. Langer's father and several companions siezed their opportunity, leaping from the train and sprinting towards some nearby woods. Over the next several months Erwin eked out a living as a labourer on farms sited many miles away from towns or even villages. Eventually he felt the danger of being picked up again to be hurled once more towards an undesirable future had passed. Erwin Langer began to make his way across Germany.

By September 1946 he had made his way to Anhausen, a village some 30 miles outside Munich. A year later he met a young waitress. Four years later they married. The third of their children – and their second son – was born in Anhausen on 27 August 1957. Bernhard Langer's long, unlikely battle towards world-wide fame and considerable

Dedicated Bernhard Langer cured the "yips" to win the US Masters and the European Open in 1985. He has also won the British and Australian Masters.

Eighth European Open

fortune had begun. From the very beginning, however, golf seemed an unlikely vehicle by which he could make his way in life.

Bernard's interest in golf began because of one simple, urgent need – money. There was always a lack of the folding stuff in the Langer household and the children had to find jobs if they wanted to have any of life's little luxuries like pocket money. His older brother and sister solved their dilemma by caddying at Augsburg Golf and Country Club which was sited five miles away from their home. By the time he was eight years old, Bernhard also was earning his pfennigs this way.

Like many thousands of caddies before him he filled in the periods between rounds by practising with one of the two or three clubs which had found their way into the caddy shed. His ability from the start was obvious. But it was not the fact that he could actually hit the ball without too much trouble that marked this youngster out from the rest, it was his commitment to practise that impressed everyone at the club. By the time he left school Bernhard wanted to be nothing else than a golfer. He did not dare dream of being a golfer good enough to win a US Masters or a European Open; he just wanted to make a modest living from a game he had come to adore. His first job was as an assistant at Munich's biggest club and it was here that he sharpened the cutting edge of his swing so that by 1976 he felt ready to embark on his great adventure by joining the European Tour.

Money, as ever, was scarce but he was young, he was enthusiastic and his optimism soared as only a teenager's can when he made his way down the Mediterranean coast and the opening events of the 1976 Tour in Portugal and Spain. But after just three tournaments he was plunged into a major crisis as his putting stroke disintegrated. It was a problem that was to remain with Langer for years. He has never really had a problem with long putts but throughout the 70s he struggled to overcome the 'yips', that involuntary jab forward with the putter that usually heralds

When he did get into trouble, Langer always found a way out.

David Cannon

74

Langer is acknowledged to be one of the finest iron-players in the game.

David Cannon

the end of a career. The problem for Bernhard was that his career was only just beginning.

Normally the 'yips' appear as a golfer grows older and the nerve endings fray as part of the natural ageing process. It is almost unheard of for a teenager to suffer from the disease. Ironically, as Langer's putting grew worse so that he seemed to be on the edge of a very public nervous breakdown, his ability to hit the ball ever closer to the flag from the fairway became even more impressive.

His reputation as an outstanding player from tee to green swept all over the European circuit. Other players drooled at his ability to strike long-iron approach shots with crisp authority and relentless accuracy. These same players then averted their eyes when Bernhard stood over the ball on the green. Advice poured in from all sides, a bewildering assortment of tips that varied from the strictly technical to the edge of the occult. In the end Langer cured his problem the same way he had caressed his talent – with hard work. He insists there was no magic cure, no

pact with anyone's devil. His will-power is such that in the end he actually willed himself to overcome the problem. It is, he admits, a problem that is never totally cured. Like an alcoholic who must avoid even one more drink, Langer realises that as far as putting is concerned he must live each day as it comes. In 1982, for example, he had serious trouble again. This time it was not the 'yips' but a decelerating stroke that left his ball wobbling short of the hole.

The cure this time was a novel one. He experimented with a change in grip, putting with his left hand below his right. It worked. There is no simple explanation why it should work. It just did. There is not even a consistent theme to where, when or how Langer grips his putter. Sometimes he putts from long range with a reverse grip and then holes out with a normal grip. It all depends on how he feels at the precise moment he stands over the ball. How well it works, however, can be seen from his career record. Certainly there is no sterner test in golf as far as putting is concerned than the steeply tilted, oil-slick greens at Augusta National

David Cannon

The West German's putting has proved a worry in the past, but at Sunningdale in 1985 most of the crucial putts dropped.

and yet it was on these most vicious of greens that he won in 1985. Within two years of his problems in 1982 Langer, astonishingly, topped the putting averages in Europe. From clown to ringmaster. And sometimes back to sad clown again.

In 1988, despite early success in the Epson Match Play Championship, the demons have been snapping at the German's putter again. By the time the Open Championship came around Langer knew that he was in real trouble once more. He worked as hard as ever under the gaze of his coach, his mentor and his friend Willie Hoffman. He tried a succession of putters, a bewildering range of models. It seemed to make little difference.

Once again Langer was plunged into the abyss. And once again there was little anyone could say. The full horror of his affliction surfaced on the final day of the Open Championship on the 17th hole of Royal Lytham. After safely negotiating the route from tee to green on this famous par 4 that dog-legs to the left, Langer stood over a putt of no more than 5 feet. From here it took him five putts to get the ball in the hole. As the ball at last dropped from view the tortured German star covered his face with his hands. If this had been anyone else but Langer then the instinct would have been to rush away to write an obituary on a distinguished career. But it is Langer and the instinct is different. He *will* recover because he will refuse to give in to the beasts that once more howl in his soul. This is the way it has been always for Langer. Show him a mountain and he will begin to plan a route towards its peak. He recognises problems but prefers to call them challenges. He is not a naturally gifted player but he is naturally inclined to work every hour available to achieve his goals in life.

He is often the first on the practice ground in the morning and last to leave at night. I have seen him experimenting with half-a-dozen drivers, a clutch of three woods and numerous wedges as he seeks perfection. He is the total professional, prepared to work harder than almost anyone

David Cannon

Bernhard Langer received a jumbo cheque from Panasonic for his well-deserved victory.

else to make himself a champion who will be respected. He is - for his dedication, his diligence, his determination, his belief in himself and what he is striving to achieve even if, at times, he seems enveloped in doubt, but then which golf professional is without doubt. Golf is such a fickle game. It is frustrating. One day you are at your best, seemingly incapable of hitting a bad shot. Every yardage is spot on; every iron crisp; every drive long and straight; every putt true. Yet 24 hours later everything can be, for no apparent reason, so wrong. It needs an iron will to cope with those form fluctuations, and the disappointments a sudden loss of form can bring. Sometimes, of course, a golfer off form will, suddenly, rediscover his touch and then the game is wonderful. Langer well knows the heights and depths golfers have to endure.

"Golf has given me more already than I ever dared wish for but it has shown me also that there is even more to aim for. It has taught me too that life can never be taken for granted, that few things are permanent," he has said. Two of the permanent things in Langer's life are his religion - he is a devout Roman Catholic –and his family. Wife Vikki and daughter Jackie, who was born in 1986, travel practically everywhere with him. They have now perfected the art of travelling with a small child and large pieces of luggage and Vikki has learned how to turn a couple of hotel rooms into a home for a week.

Vikki and Jackie have brought a contentment to Langer that was missing, but he has not changed from a hellraiser into a family man for the very simple reason that he was never the former. There may be a more modest and quiet star in some far-flung corner of the sporting universe but few of us are aware of such a man. What is nice about Langer is the fact that the man you see on the fairway is the same guy who will stand and chat to you over a glass of lager. With Bernhard, what you see is what you get. He has never had any trouble placing golf and his role in the sport in to a proper and human perspective. He does not consider himself

terribly important because that is not his nature. Some see this as proof that Langer is uninteresting. If you prefer your sportsmen to be of the school who occasionally shred hotel rooms or disappear for a few days with a bottle and a blonde then Bernhard Langer is not for you. But if you appreciate good manners and an instinctive inclination towards understatement then the German is perfect. His success on the European Tour since he broke through in 1980 with victory in the Dunlop Masters has been stunning. Only Seve Ballesteros has won more titles in Europe than Langer and together they have helped shatter the old American monopoly on real stars. What happens to Langer now and where he goes remains to be seen. He should have at least another five years during which he can continue to tilt at the more coveted titles in the golf world.

Yet, whatever the final tally, the one title that Bernhard will never lose is the title he brought with him when he first took up golf twenty years ago. You see he was, by all accounts, a nice kid back then and he is, without doubt, a nice man now . . .

August 29 – September 1, 1985
Old Course, Sunningdale Golf Club, Berkshire.

Prize money; £200,594
Par out: 35, Par in: 35, Yardage: 6,580

								£
1	Bernhard Langer	Ger.	66	72	64	67	269	33,320.00
2	John O'Leary	Ire.	68	69	67	68	272	22,200.00
3	Howard Clark	GB	66	72	68	67	273	10,333.33
	Des Smyth	Ire.	69	67	69	68	273	10,333.33
	Gordon Brand, jun.	GB	69	67	66	71	273	10,333.33
6	Ian Woosnam	GB	71	71	67	65	274	7,000.00
7	Jose-Maria Canizares	Spa.	66	71	66	72	275	4,870.00
	Severiano Ballesteros	Spa.	70	68	69	68	275	4,870.00
	Tommy Nakajima	Jap.	66	71	69	69	275	4,870.00
	Bernard Gallacher	GB	68	68	68	71	275	4,870.00
11	Wayne Riley	Aus.	70	71	67	69	277	3,680.00
12	Neil Coles	GB	70	70	69	69	278	3,096.00
	John Bland	SA	69	71	68	70	278	3,096.00
	Greg Norman	Aus.	67	68	71	72	278	3,096.00
	Mark James	GB	66	76	68	68	278	3,096.00
	Ronan Rafferty	GB	67	69	71	71	278	3,096.00
17	Carl Mason	GB	68	69	75	67	279	2,540.00
	Jose Rivero	Spa.	71	70	69	69	279	2,540.00
	Miguel Martin	Spa.	67	69	70	73	279	2,540.00
	Christy O'Connor, jun.	Ire.	71	70	70	68	279	2,540.00

Renton Laidlaw of *The Evening Standard*

Peter Urwin exhibits some style on the course as well as in the planning office.

Nobody in their right mind would want to run a golf tournament! Too may things over which the organiser has no control can go wrong. Just making sure the aspects of the tournament that can be controlled operate smoothly and efficiently cause hours of headaches, hours of sleepless nights. Yet call in at the Birchgrey office and ask any one of the half a dozen people whose job it is, under the guidance of Peter Urwin if they enjoy coping with the myriad problems that occur in running one of Europe's most prestigious events, and the answer in every case will be a resounding "yes".

Had you, in fact, popped into the Birchgrey nerve-centre just a week or so ago you might have seen Urwin pouring over a desk on which was laid out a topographical map of a golf course. Beside him on the table were a pair of scissors and a number of sheets of cardboard of various colours. Quietly he was cutting out squares and rectangles of differing size in differing colours and laying them carefully on the map to produce in the end a kaleidoscopic jigsaw.

You might be forgiven for thinking that the pressure had finally got to him but, if you knew Peter Urwin, you would know that could not be the case. He always seems to be ahead of the game. Panic is not in his nature; and why should it be with his staff and organisation? In fact the boardroom "game" he was playing was a highly serious part of the pre-planning – not for this year's event at Sunningdale, but for next year's at Walton Heath. Planning begins, incredibly but essentially, 15 months ahead of schedule. While last-minute details were being finalised for the 1988 European Open, Peter Urwin was planning the tented village area of the 1989 tournament with his tent contractor, Martin Devetta. The coloured card represented varying aspects of the village; the pieces, all cut to scale, were exactly in position.

"I have found that it is easily the best way to familiarise myself with the situation. There are more planning meetings on the ground, but at least when I get to the course I know that no tent is being pitched on a dramatic downslope or that they are being put into position over two huge bunkers," says Peter, a master of detail whose decision to go for quality in every department of the Championship has paid off handsomely.

Daniel Rose

This aerial panorama shows the final hole at Sunningdale ringed with the grandstands and the tented village neatly situated beyond.

Scaffolding is erected to support the 80,000 square feet of tentage.

If the number of corporate sponsors involved in the event has grown enormously to the extent that there are no fewer than five different "packages" on offer for the week, it is because standards are high in a field where standards are sometimes difficult to maintain. Somehow Birchgrey do and heaven help any contractor who, for any reason on the week, lets them down. The bottom line is that 80 per cent, indeed maybe even more, of the companies involved in the multi-sponsored Panasonic European Open, sign up right away for the following year. That may be the most gratifying situation of all for the Birchgrey team who are involved in the planning and designing of the tournament. There is, after all, 80,000 square feet of tentage, enough to cover Wembley football pitch five times - and it is high quality canvas built and designed to withstand the worst of all weather.

Pointing this up, Urwin recalls that similar tents to the ones now used at the European Open were in place at Wentworth last year, when the worst gales in 200 years hit the area. Falling trees rendered the course totally unplayable, signboards were blown away, flags torn to shreds, fences smashed to matchwood. Television cameras and their towers were toppled and the old-fashioned tents with guy ropes were simply uprooted. What was not affected was the hospitality tented village. The modern tents (or as they are now called, pavilions) were undamaged. That is the durability Urwin looks for in his tentage and if it looks aesthetically good too then that is an added bonus. It does. Devetta's right hand man Bill Quinn sees to that!

There is another aspect of the tented village which commands the ultimate attention of the Birchgrey team and that involves the speed with which the contractors can put up and dismantle the village. The efficiency of Devetta's operation is remarkable, especially at Walton Heath, where local bye-laws referring to the heath on which the course is laid out, insist on everything being laid out and removed within 28 days . . . in many respects a horrific schedule.

Tentage and all the necessary furniture must be booked well in advance. This is a top priority following the successful negotiations with the host club. In this respect Birchgrey have an agreement with Walton Heath and Sunningdale that runs through to 1992. Talks on the future of the event after that will begin as early as 1990. Tentage costs £215,000 this year with all the trimmings. Properly laid floors, chandelier lights, high-quality furniture. "We could reduce the figure dramatically by cutting back on comfort and spaciousness and lighting but that would defeat the whole object of the exercise which is simply to make our event the best of its kind," says Urwin, who must have contingency plans to cope with either bitterly cold or steamingly hot weather. "We never know whether we will be wanting air conditioning in the tents because of bright sunshine or heaters because of bitter winds and rain. We solve the matter by having both available. It is what our clients have come to expect.

Weather is, of course, the one factor in the complicated equation each year that Birchgrey cannot do anything about . . . except they do in a financial sense. Overall insurance for the tournament includes public liability for tents and their contents and for cancellation for unnatural reasons, but can also include some special "extra cost" policies taken out after Urwin has had consultations with the weather men at Bracknell. It is possible to insure against a specific amount of rain falling at any one time during the four days - rain so heavy as to incur additional costs mopping up or laying new 'trakway' over the resultant mud. This insurance can be handled much nearer the time of the event. It comes much later in the programme of events which are shrewdly geared to ensuring everything is perfect during tournament week.

Sorting out the tented village early means that Birchgrey can establish a year in advance just how many hospitality units they can provide the following year - an important consideration when the selling of those units will occur at the previous year's event! Getting this detail right early means that the design and printing of the tournament's publicity brochures can go ahead and this involves more round the board discussion on costings. The financial aspects of hiring packages for 1989 at Walton Heath have all been thoroughly discussed and fixed a year ahead of schedule... and this adds to the professional image the tournament and its organisers enjoy.

Of course, the European Open is fortunate in having Sunningdale and Walton Heath as its now regular venues. They meet all the features required to make a tournament successful - good road communications and access, availability of ground for parking, adequate local hotel accommodation, good on-course practice facilities, good spectator viewing, close proximity to an international airport, an adequate area for a sensibly sized tented village, and in this respect an adequate water and sewage capacity is required. Of course, most importantly too, the two venues have a character and reputation of their own which can only benefit the status of the tournament.

Both Sunningdale and Walton Heath are well paid for the inconvenience that is caused by bringing a major event to the club every second year. The sum more than covers any lost revenue from societies who would otherwise be visiting. Relations with both clubs are both cordial. Regular planning meetings take place and both clubs' infrastructure has benefited from the relationship. At Sunningdale, Birchgrey have

These robust and durable 'pavilions' are made from high quality material which looks good as well as enabling them to withstand the worst of the English summer weather.

constructed a half-mile hardcore road from Titlarks Hill to the clubhouse, built two additional practice tees which involved installing new drains and moving 5,000 cubic feet of earth, resurfaced the car park with tarmac, provided permanent electricity and telephone cables to the tented village area and provided a new water supply to meet the demands of the hospitality area and new sewage tanks to cope with toilet needs.

At Walton Heath, Birchgrey have strengthened the road to the greenkeeper's compound, installed seven 2,000 gallon sewage tanks on the course (they looked like lunar modules before they were buried underground!) and taken a new water supply from the main clubhouse area across Dorking Road to the tented village area. Peter Urwin recalls that, when excavating the large holes for the sewage tanks, a blind lady and her seeing-eye dog headed off on their usual walk over the heath. The dog followed its usual route and was taken by surprise when it came up against the big hole in the ground. It fell in. Fortunately the lady did not. The dog was uninjured in the fall and was quickly rescued!

If organisation of the tournament begins in the June of the previous year, there is a lull when all efforts are put into that year's event ... and that means for several weeks after the Championship, too, when the site has to be cleared, the financial details completed and all the various strands neatly tied up. By November - ten months before the tournament takes place- the Birchgrey staff are ready for their first selling function. This is a lavish promotional lunch at one of the London Guildhalls. It is an opportunity to thank all those who have helped make the previous event a success and a chance to encourage the clients to stay with the Open the following year. Existing patrons are guaranteed their hospitality package until the end of December. In January any packages not snapped up, and that is not many, are offered for public sale.

Back at the Wimbledon office, arrangements are being made for the 101 things that need to be done to make the tournament a success - and between November and March (or April at the latest) everything is virtually finalised. There are the grandstands to be fixed. Around the last green at Sunningdale there is a seating capacity for about 300 people to sit and

The cars in the foreground clearly demonstrate the scale of the larger 'pavilions'.

watch the action on the one side and 1,500 above the hospitality complex on the other. At Walton Heath there are more on-course stands provided by Ron Milward and his team.

Arrangements have to be made for over 250 general signs and 150 individual corporate signs with the company logo on them. The signwriters remain on location during the event in case of emergency but this early in the year they are busy at their own headquarters. The Royal Automobile Club must be contacted to arrange for the provision in early September of directional signs to the course. Yet even early pre-planning can sometimes go wrong. One year the Automobile Association began putting the signs up on the Thursday morning of the first round, unaware that the request for signs to be erected the previous weekend were genuine enough. In fact 5,000 people were present at Sunningdale that year on the pro-am day and had no idea where to park. On another occasion when signs were put up wrongly and had to be changed, Birchgrey found nothing could be done. No one was available to effect the switch over the Bank Holiday weekend!

One unexpected problem created by the main route sign-posting is caused by those pirate hospitality operators who pitch marquees in the gardens of some of the big houses near the course at Championship time. Clearly they have no parking facility but some of the pirates intuitively or cheekily send out maps of the area showing where the official Birchgrey car parks are and try to send their clients there. If car park attendants are unusually vigilant this is the reason. Car parking space is restricted enough for Birchgrey to want to be sure that only their clients use the spots.

There is provision at Sunningdale, by using fields around the course, for 3,000 cars and for those whose park is a tidy hike from the clubhouse, buses provide a shuttle service - small ones regularly in the morning and afternoon, larger ones at night when more people are likely to be leaving the course en masse. The service costs £5,000 but is an essential part of the "on-the-ground" operation. Police traffic control is the responsibility of the county authorities but on the course and in the grounds police and security services are paid from the Birchgrey budget.

Police facilities on site and security guard cover is extensive but each year something, somehow goes missing. Says Peter Urwin: "At the start of the tournament there are 200 television sets around the complex providing the on-course news service operated by Viewpress and the closed-circuit BBC coverage. By the end of the week there are usually 195!"

One year a friend of promoter Urwin remembers watching a gent in a pin stripe suit walking out with a set in his arms!

Because of the possibility of damage to the course - especially the greens -overnight there are regular patrols during the hours of darkness. Nothing is left to chance.

All these services are fixed up in the early spring when the printers are contacted to provide £8,500 worth of badges. There can be 150 different types allowing specific access to specific areas of the complex. Each day has a primary ticket colour which is changed each year to prevent, as far as it is possible, anyone trying to get in fraudulently.

The courtesy car service will have been finalised too - Mercedes Benz provide the luxury cars and overland vehicles and Birchgrey provide the attractive hostesses to drive them. Arrangements are made at a local garage for regular refuelling on account. There are hotels to be booked up too and this can prove more difficult

A view from one of the upper tiers of the grandstand shows that there isn't much room to hook the approach to the green.

when the event is being staged at Sunningdale and it clashes with the Farnborough Air Show.

Some years ago the company agreed to pass over the merchandising of souvenirs to the Sunningdale professional, Keith Maxwell. He has extended the range of mementoes to include crystal paperweights, club covers and golf bags. There are the usual items too - umbrellas, caps, sweaters, bag tags - but one souvenir is still handled by Birchgrey. That is the gift the patrons get - in 1988 it was a rather special briefcase.

Briefcases fit in to the image of the tournament and the clientele it attracts - the high-powered successful businessmen from the City of London. In fact, uniquely, there is a Birchgrey Business Club - amusingly the BBC for short but with no connection to the organisation which provides the television and radio coverage of the event each year! If you happen to see Peter Alliss in the Club tent swapping a yarn or two with some old friends it is because he has been invited. They are not his guests despite the BBC logo just inside the little trellis fence which makes the hospitality tent look all that more attractive!

The Business Club has been highly successful with the company staging a pro-am early in the year to encourage the "one big family" atmosphere and later inviting everyone to a day at the tournament venue. Anyone who takes even just

one day's sponsorship automatically becomes a member receiving regularly well-produced newsletters letting them know exactly what is happening and who is joining in.

There is a BBC tie, which is not unusual, and a BBC racehorse, which is. She is called Birchgrey Lady and may yet prove to be a big winner. In midsummer, Birchgrey Lady never lacks financial support, just on occasion a little turn of speed!

In the last few months leading up to the event there are still loose ends to be tied up and advertising to be placed in the golf magazines. The tournament is not all-ticket. Spectators can pay at the gate but this side of the business hardly warrants extensive advertising at stations around London. When that was tried it was not cost-effective. It did not add on many extra at the gate. Player negotiation is about to be completed too, by, at the latest, late June – early July. International players, always a feature of the European, will have been contacted in advance, but now their signatures are needed on important contracts. It is another anxious time. The demands on the top players are immense but it is a tribute to the organisers and to the prestige in which the event is held that some of the world's leading players have competed for the title. Indeed, in 1986, Greg Norman won a £50,000 bonus for winning both the European and Open titles in the same year.

Later in July the office staff are spending days carefully sending out tickets by recorded delivery to make absolutely sure everyone gets them well ahead of schedule. It is another job that demands the utmost accuracy. One slip here and another there could seriously damage the reputation of the event in someone's eyes. There are few, if any, slips, so good is the back-up and check-up procedure. It is Birchgrey style to ensure everything is in order.

Three weeks before the event Birchgrey moves lock, stock and barrel to the portable office at Sunningdale or Walton Heath to begin the last stage of the 15-month operation. The hundreds of queries are now channelled to the portable eight-line exchange at the site. Patiently and politely the staff cope. They too are quietly excited at the prospect of seeing all the hard work now being converted into a successful tournament.

Lady chauffeurs provide transport for the players to and from the course.

84

It is now that the promoters face the harsh reality. Have their arrangements been well made or will new problems arise suddenly to make things difficult? Inevitably there are always little niggles but generally all is well. The biggest headache is the schedule. It is a time when everyone prays for good weather to make the setting-up of the tournament that little bit easier.   Once the tents and stands are up, the fire officer has to check the safety standards, much more strict now after the Bradford Football Club fire. There must be adequate emergency exits in tents, sufficient stairways in stands to allow an orderly but fast exiting of spectators if a problem arises. Everything is checked and cross-checked by the authorities. Once everything has passed his careful scrutiny, the tents can be decorated. Birchgrey spend £6,000 on floral arrangements alone during the Championship week.

The regular discussions with the host club turn more to the question of stewarding and who will be doing what, and when. Again the groundwork has been done in a thorough fashion. Club members and members from other clubs in the area are happy to do the job for a modest fee. At Walton Heath the Surrey Greenkeepers' Association helps out too. There is a veritable army of stewards with section chiefs and a general in charge of the whole, complicated operation. Stewarding is an exacting task in which patience can be tried but tempers must never become frayed. One bad steward with a loud voice, a short temper and an unnecessary military manner can harm the reputation of the whole corps! At Sunningdale everyone is handpicked for their firmness at times, of course, but mainly for their politeness.

The sixty or so radios which are used to co-ordinate the exercise are now used every minute of every day . . . or so it seems. Waste disposal experts come in ready to remove the debris promptly and effectively overnight so that all is pristine when the patrons arrive the following day. Alex Sanderson and his team who operate the best scoreboard system in the world are on site setting up their equipment, testing radios, recruiting additional staff to provide the on-course hole-by-hole service.

The family - Alex, wife June, Alan and Mark - with additionally Raymond Smith (who

Hello, hello, hello. Who's just pinched that eagle at the 10th?

The scoreboard is constantly changing, right up to the winning putt, when it stands in peace at last.

often works with BBC Radio on their commentary team),Rohan Renolds and Ted Mason, who drives the 50-foot long articulated lorry from venue to venue, have been doing the job for over 15 years. Getting staff at Sunningdale during the school holidays is tough. Alan Sanderson would say "impossible" but somehow it all works smoothly. At least at Sunningdale the family will not be faced with the unexpected problem that cropped up at Turnberry during the 1979 European Open. Scores from the 9th - the hole out beside the lighthouse - dried up. The operator could not be raised. Worried in case he had fallen ill, Alex jumped in an electric buggy to investigate. He found the scorer quietly fishing off the rocks!

Mind you, worse has happened. There were reports one year that the 18th hole approach board was not being operated efficiently. Alan Sanderson recalls, "We were told that someone was fooling around and it seemed that way. The names of the players were all jumbled up. The operator had passed the stringent Sanderson test which proved they could read, write and work with

Behind the Scenes

A delicious lunch rounds off the morning's golf.

figures. What the test had not been able to discover was whether or not the person being employed was dyslexic!

The trophies will by now have been delivered, including the impressive main trophy – designed by Garrard, the Crown jewellers, to reflect the European nations involved in the circuit each year by including on it the flags of them all. It is unique. It is highly suitable for a championship with such stature. Incidentally a replica is produced every year for the winner with the flag of his country in enamel placed on it.

Lorry-loads of 'trakway' have been laid but more is kept on standby behind the scenes in the event of heavy rain - the one thing even Birchgrey cannot control. It is cheaper to keep it on the lorry than lay it just in case. The laying is a tedious business which curiously no one seems to have tried to improve.

When the mobile banks and exhibitions start arriving, and finally the players, all the hard work is nearly over . . . but there are still some important things to do. A check must be made to ensure there is a suitable medical presence to cope with accidents in the village or on the course. In this respect the European Open created a first in 1982 when the medical men and women were issued with bleepers that did not bleep . . . just in case they put a player off when he was putting. They worked by pressure. When the medical expert was called he or she was aware of a tingling on the skin as the pager operated.

There are final discussions with the club and main sponsor Panasonic, who will have put up all their banners at the most strategic points on the course, but not so blatantly as to affect the television coverage. There is a strict guideline on the number of banners that can be placed on televised holes and where they can be placed.

The staff may be tired but as the big day approaches the adrenalin flows. If the planning has been done correctly then all should run smoothly. All through the operation there have been regular checks and cross-checks with the PGA European Tour on whose circuit the European Open is such an important feature. There will have been hours of meetings with the PGA representative in charge of the tournament. Co-operation is total. Birchgrey rely on the expertise in many fields of the PGA; the Tour relies on the expertise of Birchgrey to run the event.

Final checks are made on the tents in the village and last-minute discussions are held with the caterers Payne and Gunter, whose job it will be to cater for 150 corporate clients in the 90 hospitality tents, with 50 more companies in the executive restaurant. Throughout the week they will provide 20,000 meals to clients and public. Alan Payne, the overall boss, has much experience in this field. His late father Gus, a remarkable character, was the man who developed the tented village complex in the 60s with the late Binnie Clark at the Senior Service tournaments in Scotland. The idea has worked well. Such is the thoroughness of the Birchgrey operation that George Griffith's team of manageresses will check each hospitality unit every 30 minutes to ensure all is running smoothly. One final check is made on the huge tented press room where newspapermen from all over Europe will converge for the week, to make sure that it is in order. With modern technology the demands of the sportswriter for electrical points and more and better lighting to allow the effective use of electronic machinery have meant the tents have become far more sophisticated.

And then it is pro-am day and the tournament is set to start. The PGA starter Ivor

Tables are laid, ready and waiting for an influx of hungry golf fans in one of the "pavilions".

Robson will begin his day-long vigil on the first tee. Four days later, hopefully, with no delays it will all be over. The winner will have been crowned and attended the celebration party, where the champagne flows and the staff of Birchgrey can afford to relax at least for a couple of hours.

I said at the start that anyone who willingly wanted to run a tournament could be considered to be off his mind, but that is certainly not the case with the experts at Birchgrey who run their sophisticated championship with consummate skill. They make it look easy. It is not – but they

have a taste for organising events and seem to like the taste.

This year they also sponsored the European Open on the women's professional circuit. One suspects the future for Birchgrey is as bright as it is for the European Open and the European Tour, packed as it is with world stars. Golf is booming and Birchgrey is playing an important part in that boom by maintaining standards. That really is what it is all about at the end of the day – quality and the Panasonic European Open certainly has that each year.

In the comfort and seclusion of the Press tent up to the minute reports are transmitted all over the world with the aid of satellite technology.

Peter Dazeley

Gordon Richardson of *Golf Illustrated*

In 1984 Severiano Ballesteros had failed to pick up the bonus being offered for any golfer who could win the Open and the European Open titles in the same season. Sandy Lyle could not collect it in 1985, but the 1986 winner of the Open, Greg Norman, had every hope he might land the jackpot double, especially as Sunningdale has always been one of his favourite courses. Promoters Birchgrey had thought up the bonus originally to try and persuade the 1983 Open winner, American Tom Watson, to come to Sunningdale. It did not work. The European Open did not fit into Watson's schedule, much to the regret of Birchgrey who will continue their efforts to get him to play for the title at least once. The bonus idea caught on with the public and so it was continued although the next three Open winners were non-American. At least Greg Norman played full time on the US circuit and had a house at that time beside Arnold Palmer at Bay Hill in Florida. He was strongly fancied to land the jackpot but in the end he left it late as slim Hertfordshire Ryder Cup player Ken Brown made things difficult for the 'Shark'. In his *Golf Illustrated* piece that year Gordon Richardson, with a fine eye for detail, put everything into perspective:

Greg Norman is World Golf Number One - and that's official.

His victory over Ken Brown at the first play-off hole after a tie in the Panasonic European Open shot him to the top of the world rankings ahead of Seve Ballesteros and Bernhard Langer.

Golf's 'Mr Moneybags' scooped up a top prize of £35,000 plus a £50,000 bonus for completing an Open/European Open double, and that pushed his winnings world-wide to an amazing £655,000. It was not even his biggest pay day - Messrs Panasonic provided an even fatter pay cheque of $207,000 when he won their Las Vegas International earlier in the year. Yet Greg, who says he will probably go out and buy a replacement for the Ferrari he has just sold (to go with his Jaguar, Aston Martin, Rolls Royce and Four-wheel drive Jeep) insists the money at stake never entered his head:

"It is a bonus but the excitement is in winning. It's the most excited I've been since

Greg Norman may have missed the odd green but he made sure he did not miss the Birchgrey bonus!

David Cannon

Nick Faldo drives at one of the most picturesque holes on Sunningdale's Old course - the par 4 5th where you drive off an elevated tee.

coming down the stretch at Augusta in the Masters this year - I wanted to win and I was ready to win."

Victory looked a foregone conclusion from the moment he moved into the joint lead, yet Brown, whose year so sharply contrasts with Greg's, refused to give in.

The Hertfordshire man, whose earnings for 96th place in the American money league total just $67,000 (exactly 10 per cent of table-topper Norman's), bounced back after taking a fortnight's rest to nurse an injured right hand.

Brown, who had cortisone treatment before passing a 'fitness test' in a pro-am at Verulam, looked to be out for the count when he pushed his second into the heather at the 14th in round four. But he coaxed in a brave 15-footer for a birdie, then trundled in a 45-footer for a two at the next. When he bunkered his approach to the last, Norman must have wondered if he would 'do a Tway' and emulate American Bob Tway's bunker birdie to snatch victory from him in the US PGA Championship. He settled for a four and a play-off.

Wayne Riley, one of the more extrovert competitors, turned up with a natty line in headgear.

Norman's birdie four at the first extra hole in the fourth play-off in five weeks on the Eurotour clinched victory over Brown – 150th in the European money list after only two previous outings in the Four Stars Pro-celebrity event and the Open where he was back home in time to see Norman win after missing the cut.

There was a bizarre incident after Brown left his play-off hole chip 6 feet short. Norman explained: "As he got over the putt he suddenly looked up and said, 'Gosh, it's gone quiet here hasn't it'. I couldn't believe it. You don't hear a thing when you're concentrating. He obviously wasn't set. I cracked up laughing and he laughed too. In all my career I've never experienced anything like it from a man with a putt to tie a major championship. It was weird."

It is history now that Brown, after a season of struggle and toil, left that 6-footer half an inch short dead on line, but second prize of £23,310 must have been welcome indeed.

While Brown headed off north to play in the Lawrence Batley event, jet-setter Norman caught a Concorde to America to keep a company day appointment in the Carolinas. The tournament will be best remembered for

Howard Clark drove badly off line at the par 4 3rd - almost on to the Sunningdale Ladies' course!

David Cannon

Ian Mosey would have preferred to be down the left at the attractive 17th. It is all trouble down the right.

Norman's latest conquest but it will also be remembered for the dreadful weather conditions on Saturday after two idyllic days of autumnal sunshine and low scoring. The deluge struck during Saturday morning and surface water soon appeared on most greens. It was a nightmare for the green staff who had worked so hard to have Sunningdale in tip-top condition for the Championship which was attracting more and more corporate interest. As the rain lashed down, it was clear officials were fighting a losing battle with the elements. Play was first suspended, then abandoned for the day, with only half the field having completed their rounds and the leaders barely into their third circuit. The round spilled over into Sunday morning and Howard Clark made ground by

coming home in 31 for 67 and a share of the lead on 202. But he struck trouble in round four, shooting a 76 for 278 and dropping back into a share of 17th spot.

Defending champion Bernhard Langer ended in 3rd place, two behind Norman's eleven below par winning tally of 269, to pick up third prize of £13,150 and Nick Faldo, who had opened with a record 62, coming home in 29, had to settle for joint 4th place on 273 with European Master's winner Jose Maria Olazabal, whose closing 66 earned him £8,916 and pushed his top of the table earnings to £207,500. Seve fought like a tiger after slipping to a third-round 72. He had opened with three quick birdies but emerged from Saturday's weather crisis an angry man. "We should never

David Cannon

Ken Brown was bunkered at the last but still got par and earned a play-off with Norman.

Peter Dazeley

Sunningdale official Nicholas Royds gives Greg Norman advice.

have been kept out in the cold for an hour without information, and never have had to restart and play just one more hole – it was ridiculous," he complained.

Greg Norman, by contrast, kept smiling – and playing in the rain."

Norman later helped Australia successfully defend the Dunhill Cup over the Old Course at St Andrews and went on to win the Suntory World Match Play title, too, as he headed for the history books by making $1,000,000 in twelve months. It was for him a momentous year. He had suffered from the suggestions that he might not have the extra steel in his personality to win a major – an allegation he shattered at Turnberry when he tamed the Ailsa course in the July. At Sunningdale he emphasised his qualities as a competitor with special gifts. The Panasonic European Open win was all the more satisfying because it was over a golf course for which he has a great love.

Norman

Mitchell Platts of *The Times*

David Cannon

The credentials belong unquestionably to those of a sporting superstar. He is blond with rugged good looks and a magnetic personality. He revels in high-octane situations. When not driving his Rolls Royce – registration number **AUSSI I** – he sidesteps into a Ferrari or an Aston Martin.

And he hammers a golf ball harder, longer and almost always straighter than most players in the world. This, then, is Greg Norman. The archetypal model of the all-Australian sportsman with his Gold Coast upbringing, the "Great White Shark" trademark , and an unremitting penchant to entertain even when he is not wielding his driver in his hands.

He once regaled the press troops at Sunningdale by insisting that the reason he topped a drive was because a worm stuck its head out of the ground just in front of the ball as he was on his downswing!

Of course the spectators were more impressed by the manner in which Norman captured the Panasonic European Open at Sunningdale in 1986. For that he pocketed not only the first prize but also a £50,000 bonus from Birchgrey Ltd., the tournament organisers, for completing a rare double following his win in the Open Championship at Turnberry six weeks earlier.

Not that the size of the cheque is too important. You would need a fleet of accountants to examine his personal fortune. He earns upwards of $10 million each year and, perhaps as much as $20 million.

For Norman, however, the name of the game is not just making money. That is automatic. What he wants is to be remembered as one of the greatest golfers ever to stride across the world's fairways.

That should not be too difficult when no less a judge than Jack Nicklaus insists: "When Greg plays well, he plays better than anybody else."

Greg and Jack, of course, are neighbours, and good friends, living in Florida. But Jack still does not throw compliments around like confetti. He believes that Norman and Ballesteros are the two best golfers in the world today.

Greg Norman's European Open win helped him make a record $1,000,000 in one year.

David Cannon

Nicklaus, perhaps, does bask in some kind of reflected glory. He sees more than a little of himself in Norman. It is not simply the blond mane, the athletic frame and the audacious shot-maker. As Gary Player once put it: "I've only ever seen one player hit a golf ball like Greg. That was Jack in his prime."

All of which is hardly surprising as Norman modelled his game on that of Nicklaus. His so-called secret to success came from reading *Golf My Way* and *55 Ways to Play Golf* – both clawed out by "The Golden Bear". That Norman educated himself on the mechanics of the swing by first reading books can be explained by his late arrival into the game. It was not until he was sixteen, and detached from his childhood friends because the family moved from Townsville to Brisbane that he turned to golf.

His mother, Toini, was no mean golfer. So with a handicap of three she had no trouble joining the Virginia Golf Club on the outskirts of Brisbane. Even so she took Greg along for company when she went to play her first round at the new club. He caddied and afterwards hit a few shots with his mother's clubs. A star was born.

Norman's father, a mining engineer, bought him a set of clubs. Norman backed off from playing Australian Rules, and squash for that matter, and after twenty months he was down to scratch. What he lacked in touch around the greens, for that is so often developed as a youngster, he compensated for by hitting the ball prodigious distances.

In essence as a late arrival he was from the start big and strong enough to see par 4s as two-shotters. If you start the game at the age of sixteen then it is all the more important to cultivate the art of getting up and down.

What is more, Norman learned by reading the Nicklaus books the fundamental craft of hitting the ball down the line and using his body naturally. He still sets himself up with a pre-shot routine which resembles that of Nicklaus right down to eyeing the entire length of the target line. By now little could divert Norman's attention from the

Greg Norman's first instruction book was Jack Nicklaus' "Golf My Way". Now they are near neighbours and close friends in Florida.

game. His only lengthy break came when he went on a family holiday to the Great Barrier Reef where he joined the beach lifesaving school.

Otherwise Norman was on the course at sunrise, off to school, then back again until sundown. His education continued under the studious eye of Royal Queensland professional Charlie Earp. There he listened to and learned Earp's wise words and, at the weekends, spent eight hours each day practising. So it need not have come as a surprise to his parents when Norman, with a life in the Australian Air Force beckoning, refused to sign on. He turned down a career as a fighter pilot and headed straight for the fairways.

Not that Norman has missed out on the high-speed world. He has flown in a Top Gun F-16 fighter, pushed the accelerator with Grand Prix driver Nigel Mansell and declared his desire to land a jump jet on an aircraft carrier. For Norman, however, life in the fast lane mostly concerns powering 300-yard drives, watched by millions around the world, and it has never been any different.

Even when he was a trainee professional Norman was in such a hurry that he immediately found himself locked in controversy. He explained: "You had to wait three years before you could go out and play in a tournament. That was according to Queensland rules but it was different in New South Wales.

"There if you proved yourself, and passed the tests, in quick time you could get invitations to tournaments as a national trainee. So I went down to Sydney. I passed all the exams in six months – the quickest on record."

Norman won his player's card. He was ready, or so he thought, to tackle the tour. But officials U-turned and told him "No way". Then Earp intervened, Norman

David Cannon

The play-off lasted only one hole. Ken Brown's putt to go on to the next stopped on the lip.

Ninth European Open

David Cannon

Greg Norman has won trophies around the world but taking the European title at Sunningdale gave him more than financial satisfaction. He won on a course he loves.

received six tournament invites and in only his fourth outing he was a winner. The 1976 field for the West Lakes Classic in Adelaide included Bruce Devlin, David Graham, Graham Marsh and Jack Newton. Norman spread-eagled them with an opening 64 which had five times Open champion Peter Thomson, then a spectator in the gallery, crowing: "He's uncomplicated, he's enormously powerful, he's without doubt the best looking golfer I've seen in Australia . . . but I've been wrong about 21 year olds before so I say nothing more."

Thomson need not have worried. Norman followed up with scores of 67 and 66, cantered to a closing 74 and came home by five shots. His star was launched into the ascendancy but less than one week later he

came back to earth with a bump. He stood on the first tee at the Australian Open and topped his drive along the ground. This time he couldn't blame a worm – only Jack Nicklaus. The American, already a four-time winner of the Australian Open had once again been 'imported' and officials had 'rigged' the draw by pairing Nicklaus and Norman together. Norman, naturally enough, was overcome by nerves. He took 80 but their long-standing friendship began in the locker room that afternoon when a few soothing words from Nicklaus served to pacify the frustrated Australian.

"Jack made me feel so much at ease," says Norman. "He said the kind of words you want to hear at that time but you don't imagine anyone actually saying to you.

Since then I've often turned to Jack for advice.''

There is no better documented case of that than at the Open Championship in 1986. Nicklaus was well aware that Norman was becoming increasingly agitated by not winning a major championship. That year Norman had led the Masters on the final day, only to lose to Nicklaus, and in June he understandably walked to the edge of the fairway to publicly rebuke an offensive spectator for calling him a ''choker'' during the US Open. That title went to Raymond Floyd. So in the dining room at the Turnberry Hotel on the eve of the last round of the Open, and with Norman ahead again for the third time that year in a major, Nicklaus moved across to the Australian. Basically Norman was told that in tense situations his left hand got too tight.

Only one person beat Nicklaus to congratulating Norman when he stood on the 18th green and savoured his sweet success. That was Laura Norman – the girl he married in 1981. Later that evening he sat with her in the grandstand above the 18th green and together they toasted life with a bottle of champagne. Back in bed daughter Morgan-Leigh and son Gregory slept soundly. Greg, too, was at peace with the world.

He was, of course, to lead the US PGA Championship the next month and to have that title stolen from him when Bob Tway holed a bunker shot at the 72nd hole. That coined the phrase ''The Saturday Slam''. Norman had in 1986 led each of the four major championships going into the final round. That, surely, deserved praise but some observers wanted to bury him for losing three and winning only one. He was naturally disappointed by that reaction although he would not have been surprised. Anyway it did not really matter. ''Who wants to live in the past,'' he argued. ''I had a great year. I won the Open. All this 'choking' talk is nonsense.''

What mattered most is that Norman used it as part of the learning process. For instance when Tway produced that killer-strike in the US PGA, Norman was composed

within minutes. Likewise when Larry Mize chipped in to land the US Masters in 1987 so Norman digested the disappointment.

Back in the clubhouse he turned on the old humour and showed why he has character, sackfuls of the stuff, as well as class. He has discovered the tough way that golf's peaks and troughs are as unpredictable as the British weather. Sadly he suffered another cruel blow when he damaged his wrist during the US Open – so he missed the Open at Royal Lytham and St Anne's as Seve Ballesteros won.

What the injury did do was give him the chance to spend a few extra weeks at home. He enjoys family life and, as every superstar should know, kids have a way of bringing instant tranquillity. Within minutes of that Masters defeat in 1987 a broad grin swept across Greg's face as he bent down to pick up Morgan-Leigh and she whispered ''I know you didn't win today, Daddy, but can we still have a party?''

September 11-14, 1986
Old course, Sunningdale Golf Club, Berkshire.

Prize money; £210,418
Par out: 35, Par in: 35, Yardage: 6,580

								£
1	Greg Norman*	Aus.	67	67	69	66	269	35,000.00
2	Ken Brown	GB	67	67	68	67	269	23,310.00
3	Bernhard Langer	W. Ger.	69	68	66	68	271	13,150.00
4	Severiano Ballesteros	Spa.	64	72	72	65	273	8,916.67
	Nick Faldo	GB	62	72	71	68	273	8,916.67
	Jose-Maria Olazabal	Spa.	68	67	72	66	273	8,916.67
7	Rodger Davis	Aus.	71	67	69	67	274	5,775.00
	Peter Fowler	Aus.	65	68	73	68	274	5,775.00
9	John Bland	SA	68	72	67	68	275	4,253.33
	Bernard Gallacher	GB	65	68	73	69	275	4,253.33
	Miguel Martin	Spa.	67	72	67	68	275	4,253.33
12	Bill Longmuir	GB	71	70	69	66	276	3,413.33
	Ian Mosey	GB	70	65	70	71	276	3,413.33
	Emilio Rodriguez	Spa	68	71	70	67	276	3,413.33
15	Jeff Hawkes	SA	70	70	68	69	277	3,020.00
	Sandy Lyle	GB	66	72	71	68	277	3,020.00
17	Hugh Baiocchi	SA	69	71	72	66	278	2,635.00
	Howard Clark	GB	67	68	67	76	278	2,635.00
	Vicente Fernandez	Arg.	69	70	71	68	278	2,635.00
	Ronan Rafferty	N. Ire.	67	73	72	66	278	2,635.00
	Anthony Stevens	GB	69	69	68	72	278	2,635.00

*Norman won Play-off at 1st extra hole.

Walton Heath

Peter Haslam, Editor *Golf World*

The great Harry Vardon, left, shows a relaxed style at St Andrews in 1927.

J. Taylor, above, three times Open Champion, joined Vardon and club professional James Braid in a grand opening match over two rounds.

It was on horseback that Herbert Fowler, designer of both the Old and the New courses at Walton Heath, first surveyed the land he was to turn into one of the finest inland courses in Great Britain. At that time it was a fairly barren sight. The heather was more than two feet high and in the few places where you could not see heather, there were giant gorse bushes. This was open heathland, once a dense forest – land that had been handed down and passed on by generations of Lords of the Manor.

At the turn of the century, it had come into the ownership of Sir Cosmo Bonsor, later to be created a baronet, and to whom Fowler was related by marriage. As Chairman of the South Eastern Railway, Sir Cosmo had been responsible for opening up the whole area for development by bringing the railway to Kingswood and Tadworth. That development would certainly be enhanced by the creation of a golf course, and therefore Mr Fowler was given his chance.

England at that time was going through something of a golf boom. Fowler, like that other great course designer, Harry Colt, had given up his law practice to concentrate on golf course design. It was also the time when it was realised that sand and heather was ideal for golf. In the case of Walton Heath, the sheer beauty of the land and the fact that it was 700 feet above sea level, where the wind would always be a factor in shot-making, made it doubly so.

He began his inspection in 1902. By August the following year, the course had been seeded and by the spring of 1904 it was ready for play. They worked hard in those days, with picks, shovels and horses and carts.

But even before the course opened, the newly formed golf club signed on its professional. James Braid, who had won the Open Championship, his first, at Muirfield, in 1901, heard about the development taking place. At that time he was in his early 30s and was the professional at Romford, Essex. He went to Walton Heath, made his own enquiries, liked what he saw and heard and, in January 1904, he signed a contract to become the professional there, with effect from May that year. It was the beginning of a partnership that was to last for nearly 50 years.

Harry Vardon, the reigning Open Champion, and J.H. Taylor, who had already won the Open three times, were invited to join the home professional, Braid, in a grand opening match. Various Members of Parliament were among the large crowd which saw the Great Triumvirate do battle over two rounds on Fowler's new creation. Vardon eventually won, beating Braid by three shots and Taylor by six over a course measuring 6,300 yards. The total prize-money, for inarguably the three best golfers in the world that day, was £105. At that time, members annual fees at Walton Heath were five guineas for men and two for ladies.

No mean golfer himself, having played for England, Fowler had built a course that was going to last. It has stood the test of time. A few of his cross bunkers may be rather out-dated now with the ball being knocked farther than he could ever have envisaged but, to all intents and purposes, what you see at Walton Heath today is what he created.

That first exhibition match, on the opening day, also set the tone. There were to be many more, including the Henry Cotton versus Densmore Shute match in 1937 and, in the following year, the Cotton and Reg Whitcombe match against Locke and Brews.

1904, then, saw the successful opening of the golf course and the launch of the Golf Club Company. It was in the following year that George Allardice Riddell, later Sir George and then Lord Riddell of Walton Heath, entered the scene. He was Managing Director of the *News of The World* Company and, as one of the founder members of Walton Heath, who had been present when Braid signed his contract, Riddell saw possibilities for his business and his relaxation interests to combine.

Together with two friends, he bought the golf club company and he took a leading hand in managing its affairs for almost 30 years. A new 9-hole course was built in 1907 (consisting of the first four and the last five of the present New course). By this time, membership had risen to 500 with over half the members having addresses in or around central London. Special tee times were set aside for them on Sundays, adjusted to suit the arrival of trains from the capital.

Henry Cotton, above, and Bobby Locke, below, played an exhibition match at Walton Heath in 1937.

Walton Heath

Right, the Prince of Wales, (later the Duke of Windsor) poses with Lady Astor after their match in 1933.

Far right, the Duke of York (later to become George VI after the abdication of his brother, the Prince of Wales), shared his brother's love of the game of golf.

Edward Lutyens, later to be knighted, who was establishing himself as one of the great architects of the day, was commissioned to design and build a Dormy House, with sixteen bedrooms, four bathrooms and a sitting room. Members were allowed to join the Dormy House Club where a room, with a bath, for the night, cost five shillings a day.

Walton Heath became the "home" club of Cabinet Ministers, politicians and journalists. The Press Golfing Society had played there since 1905 and still plays there today. The House of Commons team played there from 1907, and by 1913 there were 24 MPs and 21 members of the House of Lords among the Walton Heath membership. Winston Churchill, who joined in 1910 when he was Home Secretary, was one of them. He was made an honorary member in 1913. Another honorary member was W.G. Grace. Between 1905 and 1910, James Braid,

Not many golf clubs can claim a Dormy House designed by Sir Edward Lutyens, above, the foremost architect of his day.

from his base at Walton Heath, went out to win four more Open Championships and a host of other titles. The club's fortunes continued and in 1910 Fowler started work adding a second nine holes to the New Course, which was completed three years later.

With the outbreak of the First World War competitive golf came virtually to an end. It was not until 1919 that the *News of The World* Match Play Championship, first played at Walton Heath in 1905, returned to the course. Years later, in 1927, at the ripe old age of 57, James Braid made a valiant attempt to win the title for the fifth time. He reached the final, but lost to Archie Compton.

Before then, the club received Royal patronage when His Royal Highness the Prince of Wales (later the Duke of Windsor) played the course regularly. In 1921 he accepted an invitation to become an honorary member. A similar invitation was also accepted by the Duke of York (later King George VI). One particularly memorable year was 1933 when the Prince of Wales reached the semi-final of the Parliamentary Handicap. Against him was Lady Astor. Huge crowds turned out to watch the encounter and, after being two down at the turn, HRH won by 2 and 1. He later lost in the final.

When he died in 1934, aged 69, Lord

Riddell owned 83 per cent of all the shares in the club. He virtually owned the whole thing. It was no surprise when he asked that his ashes should be scattered over the course.

In 1935, Sir Emsley Carr, former Editor of the *News of The World* headed a consortium which bought the club. Everything was re-structured and His Royal Highness, the Prince of Wales, became the first Captain of the Walton Heath Golf Club. When Sir Emsley Carr died in 1941, the shares held by him were transferred to the *News of The World* and this became the first step in the newspaper acquiring the whole of the golf club.

This state of affairs lasted until 1970 when Rupert Murdoch took over at the *News of The World*. The game of golf did not feature in his way of life and he let it be known that Walton Heath was not wanted. The members clubbed together and bought it for £262,000. For the first time it became a members club with the management in the hands of an elected committee.

Herbert Fowler, the grand designer, died in 1941 at the age of 85. He was always proud of what he had created at Walton Heath. Nine years later, on 27 November, James Braid died, having earlier that year failed to beat his age of 80 with his score on his birthday round. He failed by just one shot.

Walton Heath today remains as they would have wished to remember it, a splendid tribute to great men and a great game. The M25 has made a noisy intrusion and, to make way for it, the 8th and 9th holes on the Old course had to be altered. Apart from that, the course largely remains as Fowler created it. The clubhouse has undergone numerous alterations since being built in 1903 and one room in it is now dedicated to James Braid. The *News of The World* Match Play Championship has passed away, but, in 1978 and 1980 Walton Heath played host to the European Open and in 1981 to the Ryder Cup.

More great golfing chapters will be written at Walton Heath, venue for so many wonderful golfing moments in the past. The club is destined to prove a worthy venue for many more championships, not least the European Open now held there every second year.

Well-known for another ball game, the inimitable W.G. Grace, above, was an honorary member of Walton Heath.

The large number of Parliamentary members included Winston Churchill, below.

1987
Walton Heath

Gordon Richardson of *Golf Illustrated*

David Cannon

No Englishman had won the Panasonic European Open title until Paul Way came along somewhat surreptitiously in 1987 and landed a title as big as the PGA Championship he had won two years earlier after playing off with Sandy Lyle. Then, he had been on top of his game but what made his Walton Heath victory in 1987 so amazing was his pre-tournament form. It had been bad but he felt at home on a course he knew well and the confidence oozed back . . . as Gordon Richardson recalled in *Golf Illustrated*:

What mixed feelings Ryder Cup captain Tony Jacklin must have had as he talked BBC viewers through Paul Way's epic comeback victory in the 1987 Panasonic European Open at rain-washed Walton Heath. He could not hide his pride and pleasure at the spectacular return to form of the 24 year old who performed so heroically for him in the Cup near-miss in Florida in 1983 and in the historic triumph two years later. But his joy was tinged with regret that Way's thrilling £36,000 victory came a fortnight too late for him to be considered for a third Cup outing at Muirfield Village.

Way displayed all his famed fighting qualities as he got the bit between his teeth to fire a brave closing 67 - incredibly his first sub-70 score of the season - for a nine below par 279 and a two-stroke win from South African John Bland and Gordon Brand, jun., who unashamedly embraced his great friend at the finish. It was a rags-to-riches story of heroic proportions for the young man from Kent.

After winning the PGA Championship and finishing 10th in the 1985 money list despite a late summer slide as he postponed an operation to have his tonsils and adenoids removed, Way made only four half-way cuts in an horrific 1986 season that saw him plummet to 125th in the money list with only £7,638 - exactly one tenth of his official earnings twelve months before.

The summer of 1987 had been no better: thirteen cuts missed, a highest finish of 34th in the Jersey Open and 136th place in the Order of Merit going into the Panasonic European Open with a paltry £4,729 prize money - £180,000 less than table-topping Ian

Surrounded by the hospitality units so much a part of the golfing scene these days Paul Way, the eventual Champion hits his shot at the short 17th.

102

David Cannon

Greg Norman recovers well from an awkward lie in the Walton Heath rough.

Woosnam, the other half of the famous Way-Way and Woosie Ryder Cup double-act in the 1985 Cup match at The Belfry.

Only once did the hero of 1985 hit the headlines - when he took ten at the last in the Dunhill British Masters second round at Woburn after playing his way into contention. So it was no surprise that the bookmakers that week at Walton Heath rated the blond Way an outside chance to win the title. Indeed, he was realistically an outside chance to make the cut.

It was a sad situation for a young man who had, as a teenager, qualified for the 1980 Open at Muirfield and whose PGA win in a play-off with Lyle had seemed to herald a glittering career. Yet here he was at Walton Heath struggling to find his game but pleased, at least,

to be competing on a stretch of heathland he knew well and cared deeply about. Walton Heath had always been a favourite of his and although the European Open course was a composite one incorporating some holes from the Old and some from the New course, he liked the layout.

It is difficult to imagine how he felt. The PGA win had given him ten years' exemption but his pride was badly dented. Friends had rallied round but there was no early indication of heroic things to come, of a comeback so unexpected that anyone foolish enough to put a substantial wager on him would be sure to make a fortune.

To be truthful, Way did nothing spectacular for two days - except that he did make the half-way cut. His first hurdle carefully manoeuvred, he could afford to be more

Tenth European Open

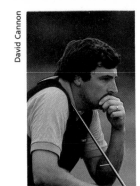

David Cannon

Caddie Peter Coleman looks on (at top) as his "boss" Bernhard Langer recovers from the rough while (above) Derrick Cooper pensively considers the line of his next putt.

German slipped on the last day to a 75 and it was Way, against the odds, who came through.

A series of brave putts and a near ace at the 9th where he hit a 4-iron to 12 inches, were the key to victory after overnight leader Bernhard Langer faded, following a triple bogey seven at the 4th. Langer lost a ball off his recovery after hooking his drive, dropped back under penalty and then re-dropped. Tournament official Mike Stewart told him the second drop (Langer thought his ball had rolled nearer the hole) was illegal under the lost ball drop regulations, which stipulates it should simply be dropped as near as possible to the point from which it was struck. He received a second penalty point for picking up a ball in play and had Stewart not swiftly intervened to order him to replace his ball the West German would have been penalised a third time for striking it from the wrong place. Said a philosophical Langer: "In golf you learn something every day".

Bland and Brand jun., earned £18,600 each and Brand finished top man among the final qualifiers for the Equity and Law Challenge with 339 points from 311 birdies and fourteen eagles, twenty points ahead of Sam Torrance with 331 points.

Brand, jun., would not win the Equity and Law Challenge which captured the imagination of the public. Barry Lane would take the top prize in the 36-hole finale at Royal Mid-Surrey. Ted Dexter, the former England cricket captain and a man dedicated to producing bright new talent in cricket and golf, had thought up the idea to create a vehicle which would encourage attacking play – and it had worked. Way might not have been high on the list at the end of the season but he had attacked all through the European and come through with all guns blazing. It was a remarkable performance.

A brilliant last round 65 from Ian Woosnam strengthened his lead at the top of the money list as he took fifth place, a stroke behind Christy O'Connor jun. The little Welshman passed on the credit to defending Champion Greg Norman who gave him a five-minute putting lesson: "He told me to get my hands forward and keep the face shut on the putter, and to keep it low going through." Ironically,

adventurous over the last two rounds – but victory? With Greg Norman, Lyle, Ballesteros, Faldo and Bernhard Langer in the field you had to be dreaming of a fairy-tale victory if you were prepared that grey, rainy week to back Way, and fairy-tales do not often happen in golf!

Jose-Maria Canizares had jumped into the lead early on with a five under par 67, despite the fact that he was still troubled by a rib injury which had effectively killed his chances of making the Ryder Cup again. It had troubled him all season. Canizares, bearing the pain, led by a shot from Robert Lee, on the first day. Way was three back – an encouraging start but one nobody took too much notice of! Canizares slipped away, not surprisingly considering his fitness problem, with a second round 74 as Langer moved up. His 67 for 137 put him two in front of Derrick Cooper and another former winner, Gordon Brand, jun. Way shot 71. He was still only four behind. In the third round, Way shot 71 again and was three behind Langer who led from John Bland of South Africa and Brand jun., but the West

Norman himself never seriously threatened and there were disappointing showings, too, from Severiano Ballesteros, Nick Faldo and Sandy Lyle, who turned what would have been a 68 into a 71 with a 72nd hole seven.

For one player the European Open marked his retirement. Warren Humphreys, the 35 year old Kingston, Surrey, professional, who played on the winning Walker Cup side, won the English Amateur Championship in 1971 and took the 1985 Portuguese Open title decided enough was enough.

But he explained: "Things have not gone well this year and I feel it is time to strike out on another career. I have nothing definite fixed but hope to exploit some opportunities in the fringe areas of promotion, company days

and so on. I've got two children and with my son, Jason, at school, taking the family off to South Africa for the winter is no longer on."

A cruel hoaxer added to Sam Torrance's misery during the week after his Arnold Palmer blade putter was stolen on pro-am day.

Caddie Brian Dunlop left Sam's clubs in the pro shop for a few minutes while he went to the car for some grips. When he returned the putter had disappeared from the bag. Next day the club received an anonymous telephone call from a man claiming to have bought the putter from someone in a motorway service station. It turned out to be a hoax.

"It's not the putter I used to hole the winning putt in the Ryder Cup but it was very much a favourite," said Sam.

David Cannon

Paul Way prowls as Australian Rodger Davis considers the line and pace of his next putt.

Portrait of a Winner
Way

Bill Elliot of *The Star*

David Cannon

Paul Way has never tried to soft-shoe his way into the limelight. Right from the start the young man from Kent has been the sort of high-profile player you noticed even if he was three-putting a green. Short, 5 feet 8 inches, and stocky, 11 stone, Way's shock of blond hair and strutting stride marked him out as someone to watch.

He entered the pro ranks in 1981 after making his debut in the Walker Cup. Within two years he was in the Ryder Cup team which so nearly triumphed in America, partnering Seve Ballesteros and prompting Tony Jacklin to suggest that the only thing likely to mark out a boundary to Way's achievements was the lad himself. "Where he goes, what he does is up to him. If he is prepared to work at it then the world is his for the taking," grinned Jacko, who recognised within the aggressive Way's nature something close to the way he had been twenty years earlier.

As a schoolboy in Kent, Way and close friend Mike McLean had shown prodigious talent for hitting golf balls. The other demands of school life left the two mates less enthusiastic but an understanding teacher allowed them to practise while classmates were studying. The teacher did not really have a choice. Way, for sure, would have just walked out, taking his clubs with him anyway had permission not been granted. That was the way he was and it is the way he remains.

Yet at the ripe old age of 25, Paul Way is suddenly under close public and private scrutiny. In his seven years as a professional Way has shown himself to be a player capable of reaching the rarefied heights and equally adept at plunging headlong into the depths. More than anyone else in Europe, his career has been a roller-coaster ride. One year he is dancing with the angels, the next he is suffering publicly in some private hell. He does not have form; he has moments, days of brilliance and then the inspiration departs and Way looks like a stuttering shadow of the player who once had the game by the throat.

The fact is that Way's experience

Simon Bruty

When Tony Jacklin and the team returned with the Ryder Cup after that history-making win, Paul Way and girlfriend Julie went along to congratulate the boys.

Paul Way holds up his arm to ask the crowd to stand still as he prepares to hit a shot.

106

over the last couple of years has been the sporting equivalent of being led up an alley and having the living daylights kicked out of him. Only, in Way's case, the beating was not done in private. He had to suffer in full view of the public, the Press and the roving TV camera. Who needs the Roman Games when you can watch someone like Way being eaten alive by the sporting gods? And do it all from your armchair.

Until he won the Panasonic European Open in 1987, Way's fall from grace post-1985 had been spectacular. It had also been chilling and largely inexplicable. Although he turned pro in 1981 it was not until the following year that Way played full time on the European circuit. Success was, more or less, instantaneous. He won the Dutch Open and finished the year in 30th place on the money list. At twenty years of age he was hailed as the greatest prospect to hit British golf for many years.

It was not just the fact that Way had won. It was his whole manner. He *looked* good and he talked well. There was a natural swagger about him that was appealing both to the punter and the connoisseur. Sport loves a good ''little un'' and it relishes even more a good young ''little un''. Way was very good news indeed and he proved he was not just an extraordinary flash in the pan when in 1983 he made the Ryder Cup side, won £43,484 in official prize-money and moved up to 11th place in Europe.

In 1984 he shuffled back a little and ended the year in 26th spot but in 1985 he won the PGA Championship at Wentworth after a play-off against Sandy Lyle. He finished that year with £76,140 for 10th place and once again made the Ryder Cup side. Twelve months later he was ranked 125th in Europe. He failed to make the half-way cut in almost every event, he looked tired and he lost control on the course. It was a pathetic descent.In truth, his decline had begun almost immediately after his great triumph in the PGA Championship, but then his problems were put down to infected tonsils which sapped his strength and, ultimately, drained his confidence. No such

David Cannon

Paul's record had been dismal all season but he did little wrong at Walton Heath – and when he did he usually made par.

excuse could be made about 1986. The fact was that Paul Way had turned from a natural winner into a player apparently incapable of ever winning again.

As the weeks grew into months and the list of failures threatened his sanity, Way was plunged into the darkest depression of his life. ''I never felt so bad that I considered throwing myself off a bridge but I got pretty close to it,'' he says. ''I suppose I was as low as it was possible to get. Certainly I'd reached the point where I had to face the fact that I might have to find another way of making a living.''

Then, just as he was contemplating those options, Way found the magician's touch once more. Against everyone's expectations he won the Panasonic European Open at Walton Heath in 1987. It was a stunning return to form and it was as inexplicable as his decline had been. No one, least of all Way himself, knows why the adrenalin surged again that week.

107

Paul coaxes another putt in en route to a triumph that was just too late to help him keep his Ryder Cup spot.

David Cannon

"Yeah, of course it was a surprise to me to win that week. Why then? What had I been doing wrong before? I never thought about picking up the first prize all week. How could I? I was just trying to survive. But then I found myself ten under par with nine holes to go.

"The chance was there, the challenge was to take it and the alternative to winning just did not bear thinking about. I knew that with one win I could be free of the terrible times but I had to prove it to myself. Every shot carried with it a possible disaster. No, I wasn't nervous – it went beyond that. Far beyond. A few months before I'd been thinking: 'Christ, I may have to give this game up because it's costing me too much money'. Now suddenly I was in pole position again. I'm proud of the way I played those nine holes. I had to dig down deep and I achieved something very important. It could easily have all gone wrong and I might never have recovered from that you know."

Instead, of course, it all went right for Boy Wonder. And then it all went wrong again. Friends of Way – and he has many– had hoped that victory in the European Open would re-ignite the talent that had once threatened to burn his name into the game's most glittering pages. It has not. Life since Walton Heath has not been as bad as the really bad times for Paul, but it has not been that good either. The anticipated comeback has not been sustained.

Now time is running out again. And yet it would take a brave man indeed to write off this intriguing and sometimes compelling golfer. Surely no one can be as good as Way has been and then lose it all? There are those who believe he had it all too quickly, that success blunted his enthusiasm for the battle and, more importantly, for the practice necessary before battle. Others point to his love of the good life, his need to jump into a fast car and head for the hottest disco in town – but is this really wrong for a young man with money in his pocket and an understandable disdain for carpet slippers and the fireside?

Certainly Paul himself is far from ready to throw in the golf towel just yet.

"After Walton Heath I reckon I can win anywhere, anytime. Maybe I had been a little too complacent before, maybe all the success had come too quickly. If I've learned anything from the last few years it is to savour the moment, to relax and enjoy what I'm doing today and allow tomorrow to take care of itself."

It does not mean, however, that Way has ceased to make any plans for tomorrow or the day after that. He spent the winter in South Africa, partly to practise in the sun, but also to mould himself into the sort of sharp physical shape necessary these days to play golf in Europe. Hard work has never bothered Way, at least not when it is work he enjoys. So he had a South African Army friend of his, a physical training instructor, work out a training regime that would impress even the likes of Daley Thompson. After a few months of graft, including doing 150 press-ups three or four times a week,

Way is back in top shape. What he must do now is to remain patient, to ignore the calls to press the panic button once more. Waiting to win anywhere, anytime, may be the way Paul Way has to play the rest of his career. He is not a candle waiting to be snuffed out in the wind.

Meanwhile, one story captures the spirit and the character of this golfer well enough. When last year's ecstatic Ryder Cup team returned to Heathrow they were delighted to see standing among all the thousands of fans, Way and his fiancée Julie Morrison.

No one expected Way to be there, leading the singing and the dancing, but there he was. It was a typical gesture on the part of this sometimes misunderstood man. It took guts to turn up at Heathrow. And it took something else as well – it took class. It takes the same two things to win golf tournaments. Guts and class – Paul Way has them both.

September 10-13, 1987
Walton Heath Golf Club, Tadworth, Surrey.

Prize money; £221,908
Par out: 36, Par in: 36, Yardage: 7,108

								£
1	Paul Way	GB	70	71	71	67	279	36,660.00
2	John Bland	SA	69	72	70	70	281	19,100.00
	Gordon Brand, jun.	GB	70	69	72	70	281	19,100.00
4	Christy O'Connor, jun.	Ire.	70	70	72	70	282	11,000.00
5	Ian Woosnam	GB	73	71	74	65	283	9,320.00
6	Neil Coles	GB	71	70	75	68	284	6,180.00
	Mark Mouland	GB	71	72	72	69	284	6,180.00
	Greg Norman	Aus.	71	72	69	72	284	6,180.00
	Ronan Rafferty	GB	74	70	69	71	284	6,180.00
10	Jose-Maria Canizares	Spa.	67	74	78	66	285	3,738.33
	Rodger Davis	Aus.	69	71	72	73	285	3,738.33
	Nick Faldo	GB	73	73	70	69	285	3,738.33
	Bernhard Langer	W. Ger.	70	67	73	75	285	3,738.33
	Robert Lee	GB	68	72	76	69	285	3,738.33
	Wayne Westner	SA	72	73	73	67	285	3,738.33
16	Severiano Ballesteros	Spa.	70	71	75	70	286	2,866.00
	Gordon J. Brand	GB	71	75	72	68	286	2,866.00
	Howard Clark	GB	70	74	72	70	286	2,866.00
	Brian Marchbank	GB	75	71	73	67	286	2,866.00
	Des Smyth	Ire.	69	75	73	69	286	2,866.00

View from the box

Renton Laidlaw of *The Evening Standard*

Renton Laidlaw.

I cannot quite remember whether it was at Sunningdale during the European Open or not, but then I have tried to put this embarrassing moment out of my mind.

I was commentating with John Jacobs on a particularly brilliant run by Australian Greg Norman. He had had a string of birdies and as he lined up what was going to be fourth in a row, I suddenly felt very dry in the throat. Now television commentators are pampered. There is a back-up staff that caters for their every whim and request, even while they are on air. The technicians provide a microphone cut-off button that allows the commentator to speak to the director without being heard by the viewer. It is fiendishly simple and only requires the commentator to press a small red button on a small black box. The red button. Not the white button which allows him to speak to the overall producer, the blue button that, to all intents and purposes, did nothing at all. As I built up the drama of Norman's latest birdie putt, I leaned over to the control panel and pressed the button that should have cut me off. Using, thankfully, the most polite language, I pleaded for some tea and scones. Norman holed the putt and when the applause had died down the director told me that the tea was on its way but that, in future, would I not make the request publicly to millions of viewers around the country. Yes, you guessed it - I had pressed the wrong button. I never asked for tea ever again.

Commentating just bristles with pitfalls. The job, on the face of it, is a simple one - to flesh out the pictures on the viewer's screen at home, impart additional relevant information you usually have at your fingertips, clearly, lucidly and if possible before the picture on the screen changes to another subject! Easy - well it would be, if it were not for the fact that as you chatter on it is more than likely that the director is already talking you through the next shot!

And if the commentary box happens to be up on stilts with a clear view of the hole, you are describing, the rule is never, ever to take your eyes off the screen. More than once a commentator has, to his great embarrassment, been caught out, describing what he was looking at out of the window and not what the viewer was seeing on the screen. Mind you, in the days when Independent Television covered the European Open, the commentary box was hidden in the pine trees close by the 14th ... close enough for an off-line drive to come clattering in to the compound to give the commentators the chance to do some on-the-spot work. In fact it was very useful. It is difficult to capture the atmosphere of an event fully if you are locked up (it seemed like that) in a hut in the middle of the woods talking eloquently, you hope, about one of the most beautiful courses in Britain. Mind you, another of my co-commentators at Sunningdale one year was so distressed to hear that we would have to voice-over the pictures at the BBC Television Centre because of a strike, that she went to remarkable lengths to take the course with her! She solved her problem of getting properly in the mood by arriving at TV Centre carrying a large sack and golf shoes! She put on her spikes in the sound cubicle, then emptied the contents of the sack on to the carefully scrubbed floor. Technicians, used to keeping the equipment in pristine dust-free conditions, blanched as she spread heather and gorse and grass all over the floor to give her the "feel" of Sunningdale and get her atmospherically in tune for her commentary. Politeness prevents my even giving a hint of who she was.

These days the BBC covers the European Open which means a busy week for Peter Alliss, Bruce Critchley, Alex Hay, Tony Jacklin, Harry Carpenter and Clive Clark, who are well qualified to explain what happens behind the scenes. The green light goes on and executive producer John Shrewsbury, the man with overall responsibility for the production, settles down with directors Alistair Scott and Fred Viner for a lengthy session.

One former executive producer called it, graphically enough "organised chaos" with the emphasis on organised. To some extent it is confusing because of the nature of the game. Golf does not happen in front of you in one place. It happens all over an area of some 150 acres. When someone holes a putt on the 6th he could tie with another player dropping a shot, at exactly the same time, on the 15th. The ever-changing leader-board means that it requires a clear-headed director with the back-up of a producer. He must really know golf to bring you not only the drama of the event as it happens, but also the feel of the tournament.

Clive Clark, for many years the BBC "foot

Bruce Critchley, foreground, with Tony Jacklin and Peter Alliss in the BBC commentary box.

Clive Clark, BBC's roving commentator follows play to all parts of the golf course.

soldier", is a man who too seldom gets the chance to commentate on a player about to hit a shot from the middle of the fairway. He is brought in only when a player has hit into the direst trouble or for the post-round interview - Clark explains that the most complicated event of all to cover is the Open where the aim is to show all eighteen holes. At the European Open, the first hole, and the six holes from the short 13th are the usual holes covered.

Clive, a former professional at Sunningdale, can often be seen with an antenna coming out of his ear. Usually he has an engineer with him to carry the microphone and in this respect was luckier than his colleague, Malcolm Gregson, who used to do the same job for ITV. At one event, Gregson and another ITV stalwart, John Helm, who learned the ropes at BBC Radio, were sharing a microphone as they operated on parallel holes divided by a row of trees. When Gregson was suddenly called in to do an interview, the technicians could not understand why they were getting no sound, until they realised that he was not holding the microphone (Helm had that 130 yards away!). Malcolm just appeared to be. The "mike" was in fact the handle of his umbrella!

You can imagine the reaction in the mobile control room, or, as it is better known - the scanner. This is a huge vehicle, packed with all the sophisticated equipment that is required to mount a full outside broadcast. It is a studio on wheels ... with a flight-deck-style operations room that puts Concorde to shame!

It is in the scanner that everything happens! The producer, in overall executive charge; the director, responsible for choosing the pictures the viewer sees at home; the vision mixers; the production assistant who maintains a stop-watch timing of the programme; plus all the sound and vision control technicians. All are there, operating a mass of controls in front of a bank of 40 monitors which can show the pictures from up to 34 cameras on the course. Pictures can be cut in half, superimposed, flipped or shot off into the corner of the screen by just one piece of complicated equipment. The van has miles of wiring but amazingly little goes wrong, although on one occasion, as I waited up a tower at West Kilbride for the start of a transmission from the PGA Seniors, I was shocked to hear that the scanner had caught fire. As black smoke began

seeping through between the monitors, the production assistant, showing all the dedication of her craft, continued the countdown to the start of the programme as many of her colleagues leapt to safety! As luck would have it my microphone stayed live and we did have pictures from an on-course unit. We went on air bang on time with nobody at home aware of the behind-the-scenes drama.

The ability to remain calm in a situation like that is the trade mark of the BBC chief commentator Peter Alliss, who learned so much about the skills of the job from the late Henry Longhurst, a man who knew how to use silence to great effect. Henry, who had been involved in the very first outside broadcast from a golf event just before the war, is still remembered fondly today for his pithy comments and well-chosen remarks. He has the ability to say, in an instant, what others might have thought of saying too late.

Alliss calls the commentary box "the potting shed" and it is there that the team put words to the pictures fed them from the scanner, and where Harry Carpenter (or sometimes Steve Ryder) do their second-perfect links into "Grandstand" or the recorded highlight programmes. That is another highly skilled operation usually completed under pressure and sometimes with a considerable amount of distraction. On one memorable occasion I was with Harry in the commentary box built on stilts beside the 17th green on a wind-lashed Turnberry course in Scotland. It was autumn and play had been completed - but only just - as the equinoctial gales made conditions not just tricky but virtually impossible for the professionals. Gary Player inevitably had been one of the few to master the conditions. It was just the sort of challenge he loves. While others virtually gave up the unequal struggle, Player battled on relishing the chance to take on and beat the elements. I had taken him out to be interviewed by Harry for the highlights and had difficulty in getting into the commentary box as the wind was so strong. Once in, and with the wind howling outside, we felt rather the way Captain Scott and his polar adventurers must have felt when they huddled together for heat as storms raged outside their small tents. It was rough. Harry, as always, was his usual calm self. He put Gary at ease and the huge arc-lights were switched

Peter Alliss has equal measures of experience and knowledge to inform and entertain.

View from the box

The nerve centre: the 'Scanner' or control room, where the producer decides where the best of the action is to be found.

on, giving the whole scene a surrealistic look. The floor-manager, a slim, sensitive, artistic-looking young man signalled one minute to go to Harry who was adjusting his tie. The countdown had reached 30 seconds to "on-air" when the flimsy walls of the commentary box began to creak and bend inwardly in the wind. Crew members rushed to prevent an implosion as Harry began his interview. One wall was particularly shaky and five of the BBC's strongest "stage-hands" were having to hold it in position. A light was nearly knocked over as more people rushed to help hold the wall in place. The door swung open and another technician rushed to close it again as the howling wind swirled round the inside of the fragile structure. Harry and Gary did a remarkable job. They continued their chat as if nothing was happening, Gary making the point that in his whole careeer he had never played in worse wind conditions than he had that day. Viewers at home were unaware of the drama being enacted just three yards from where the interviewer was standing. It was a classic case of the show must go on . . . a tribute to the professionalism of all involved in the golf coverage.

It is so easy to criticise, and viewers are so ready to do it, but following a golf ball on a telephoto lens against a grey-white sky is never easy. The regular cameramen either on BBC or with the Trans World crews do a remarkable job. Believe me, *they* get annoyed if, for any reason they lose the ball in the air. One cameraman a few years ago was more annoyed than usual. Having lost it, he stepped back from his expensive camera and the ball hit him as it crashed down-to-earth badly off line! Being a golf unit cameraman and having to cope with our weather is a job which demands stamina. Out on a tower or, even worse, strapped in on the platform of a "cherry picker" - the high crane 100 feet above the ground - on a wet, cold, windy day (and there are plenty of them on the European Tour) is not pleasant even in short bursts. When the roster calls for a cameraman to be on duty for several hours in his exposed spot it is a wonder he does not catch pneumonia!

They are dedicated men, however, always keen to bring the viewer the pictures that matter during any transmission. Mind you, one cameraman was somewhat embarrassed at a tournament when he carefully followed a professional into the bushes to look, the cameraman thought, for his ball. The director was of the same view. "Give me a close-up . . . quickly, quickly," he requested. The cameraman focused in smoothly only to discover that what had taken the pro into the bushes at a spot he thought was well out of the public gaze was the call of nature! There was a frantic change of picture before anything untoward happened!

While the television men are busy in action so, too, is the BBC Radio team which brings coverage of every PGA European Tour event during the season. John Fenton is the long-serving expert.

Until a few years ago, getting to the radio commentary position was no laughing matter. It is different now thanks to the work done by Henry Longhurst who insisted on a staircase being built to all commentary positions. They are called Longhurst ladders and they make it easy for the commentary team to get into position without risking life and limb. John has the best of both worlds, frequently sharing commentary with me high above the 18th green and sometimes walking with the stars to give on-the-spot reports. Sometimes he might even have the use of an electric cart and an engineer, although this sometimes can be troublesome if the engineer not normally assigned to sport, knows little about golf, cannot apparently drive a cart and has no sense of direction. It has happened on the odd occasion when all the regulars have been engaged on other outside broadcasts! It is tough for a reporter out specifically to watch every shot of Severiano Ballesteros, Sandy Lyle or Nick Faldo, if he ends up looking instead for his engineer and the equipment who appear to have disappeared into thin air. Chris Rea and George Bayley are the other men "on the ground" as was Don Mosey for many years until involved in an incident while lying on the grass at what might have been a European Open. He was commentating through the legs of the crowd, when a photographer came along, plonked down his tripod, narrowly missing Don's fingers, and then effectively screened the action from him. It was raining heavily at the time, a wind was blowing and it was cold, and the combination of all those distinctly adverse factors left Don in no two minds that it was more comfortable in the Test Match Special cricket commentary box.

The Development of  the European Tour

The Panasonic European Open is part of the sporting success story that is the Volvo PGA European Tour. The graph of the Tour over the past ten years has shown a continual upward trend - more tournaments in a longer than ever season and more money for the players to chase.

The man in charge of this complicated operation is Ken Schofield, a 46 year-old Scot who played an important role in the rescue operation that saved the European Championship, and has successfully resolved other crises in the years that he has been at the helm. Of course he is Executive Director and is responsible to the Tournament Committee led by Irishman John O'Leary, but his influence throughout has been considerable.

Since 1978 prize money has increased from £1,000,000 to £10,000,000 a season, but the real growth may be about to begin as the Tour moves into a new golf course construction programme with Alfred McAlpine and the Co-operative Wholesale Society.

Today the financially independent Tour has a staff of 30 - quite a change from the days when it was run, as a section of the PGA, by one man in a small office not far from Liverpool Street Station! The commercial expansion has been remarkable and reflects the growing status of the game especially over the last few years.

Schofield recalls that when he joined the circuit in 1973 the Tour was already two years old. In 1971 John Jacobs, the Ryder Cup golfer and respected golfing coach, had been employed to bring business methods onto the circuit and, with the help of Tony Jacklin, build a new Tour for the 80s and 90s. In four years Jacobs, at ease in the

Ken Schofield, whose vision and determination carried the European Open through its early rough ride. On his right is Sven Tumba, original instigator of the tournament concept.

The importance of world-wide TV coverage is demonstrated by the popularity in Japan of European stars. The Japanese ambassador in London, Toshio Yamazaki, shares his nation's love for the game.

boardroom discussions with the captains of industry, (most of whom wanted a lesson from him anyway if they played golf), had doubled the prize money from £250,000 to £500,000. It was at this stage that Ken Schofield took over a post he never anticipated he would fill when persuaded to leave banking in Scotland to join the George Simms Organisation in London.

Simms ran a PR organisation from an office handily situated just off Fleet Street. He was a former Press Association reporter and streetwise in the business of publicising golf events. He was the "Master" and, even now, in retirement, is held up as the expert, the man who did it best. Simms needed an assistant and scoured the country for a suitable replacement to train as his successor. One day in Edinburgh he made an appointment to meet Ken Schofield. He did not tell Ken right away but he knew he had found his man. Ken was a super-enthusiast who with his keen love of the game had spent many hours at the tournaments. More importantly he took copious notes at those events compiling, for his own amusement, unusual statistics and interesting data. Ken, who had been the youngest bank manager in the Trustee Savings Bank in Scotland, moved to London and began the adventure which today has him controlling the successful PGA European Tour, now also called the Volvo Tour after the Swedish car firm became corporate sponsors, swelling in the process the Tour's bank balance to the tune of at least £10 million.

Ken's involvement with golf intensified under George Simms. He became a regular press officer on the Tour and caught the eye of the shrewd Jacobs who wooed him away to join him on the circuit. George Simms was, at the one time, sad to have lost the man he felt would maintain the end of the golfing business he had cornered so effectively, yet delighted at the opportunity afforded his protégé. They are today still good friends.

Schofield recalls that in 1975 there were still some gaps to be filled on the summer circuit. The tournament players wanted to have the chance of playing each week and they did not have that luxury. The gaps were particularly troublesome to those players from overseas whose participation on the European Tour is and always has been, so welcome. The European circuit is, after all, the most international of all the major Tours. The gaps were due to the poor economic climate at the time and Schofield saw his role as simply to get them filled. He did and made another important change too.

He decided that it would be best for the tournaments to finish on a Sunday. In those days Saturday was still the main sporting day of the week, but BBC Television's Sunday "Grandstand" had started up and the producers were keen for Sunday sporting action. Golf filled the bill. Sunday finishes also gave the sponsors two weekend bites at the cherry as far as the promotion of their particular product was concerned and it paved the way for the original opening day of Wednesday to become a pro-am day. Schofield's policy, he maintains, has always been to give the best possible return for the best prize-money - prime-time television as well as extensive media coverage in the national papers. The Tour's close relationship with the BBC has been an important factor. The BBC are happy to cover European Tour events in Britain and then syndicate the programmes around the world. Japan is an important buyer. Sandy Lyle, Seve and Nick Faldo are well-known names in Japan because of the television appearances in the land where golf really has taken over as a spiritual substitute for some, and where the richest club costs £1,000,000 to join!

The BBC, who televise the European Open, signed their first £1.8 million deal with the Tour in 1979. The partnership is now secure right into the 90s. It has been mutually beneficial. There has been expansion, too, on the Continent, expansion that has further underlined the golfing family of nations that is Europe now.

Today the events on the European Tour are also sometimes covered televisually by the Trans World International section of the International Management Group, perhaps better known as the Mark McCormack organisation. It is a joint project between the Tour and the IMG to cover events mainly on the Continent and show them principally on satellite but also in various areas of Britain through the Independent Television Network. ITV abandoned golf coverage a few years ago when costs began to spiral and influential programme controllers in

Increased TV coverage demanded new angles and a closer view of the players in action. The mobile buggy enabled the camera to follow the play to the far corners of the course.

David Cannon

the various regions saw more financial benefit for advertising by showing old films on Saturday and Sunday afternoons.

There is, however, a new spirit abroad and with modern lightweight cameras and improved manning facilities, there is the chance that ITV may again become a stronger supporter of televised golf than it has been for some years. Certainly it seems a shame for the Independent Network not to cash in on the boom in the game caused by the emergence initially of Severiano Ballesteros, the reigning Open champion, but latterly of Sandy Lyle and Nick Faldo, who have also won that title, and Ian Woosnam who made more money last year than anyone else has in the history of the game. Golf, unlike many other sports, has British winners playing a vital part in the international success. The game is noted for its honesty, its sportsmanship and the good behaviour both of the fans and the players.

Ken Schofield is particularly happy that the whole golfing scene is having "such a good run" because, in one respect, it makes his job easier. It is more likely that a company will want to put money into a sport with a distinctly family orientation than one whose reputation is sullied by hooliganism or bad behaviour. He has strong views on that unsavoury aspect of sport and deplores the fact that it is sportsmen and sports-women who sometimes carry the can for the bad

behaviour of those who come to watch them.

Golf, because of the European successes on the world stage, has a high profile and keeping it there in the important corridors of power is one of the Tour's most noted vice-presidents, the former Minister for Sport Sir Neil MacFarlane. Sir Neil is the parliamentary consultant for the Professional Golfers' Association, a keen golfer whose counsel Ken Schofield and his staff value greatly. He will do even more in the future when he joins the board of Tour Properties, the company set up to liaise in the building of those new courses around the country. He is a friend of golf and in political and business terms brings his considerable qualities happily to the Tour and all it stands for.

In many respects golf has been ahead of the game as far as unity in Europe is concerned. While the talk is of a truly united Common Market in Europe by 1992, it is fair to point out that in golfing terms the continent has been united since 1972. The European Open concept and the fact that in 1979 Continental players were brought into the Ryder Cup match which had previously been purely for professionals from Britain and Ireland and America to contest, helped cement that feeling of a total camaraderie between golfing nations. This year Ballesteros returned triumphantly to Lytham, the excellent Lancashire venue where in 1977 Sven Tumba had convinced

Bob Martin

Schofield and his committee that he had the men and the money to get his European Open off the ground in England.

Today over 100 Patrons are involved in the Panasonic European Open, now firmly established on a circuit that continues to grow in almost every direction, but hopefully not so fast as to suffocate those whose job it is to run its affairs. "The challenge the Tour has," says Schofield, "is in maintaining the growth potential. As far as tournaments are concerned we have a great as yet untapped market on the Continent not least in the southern half of Europe."

The great players who have played such a vital part in the expansion of the circuit, have still more to do to keep the Tour moving forward. All over Europe new courses are being built which will encourage much more interest in the game and create demand for even more events, notably in Spain - the biggest development area.

Schofield is looking forward at some stage in the future to getting the Tour into Greece and Austria and there are high hopes of an event in the not too distant future in Finland where there is a keen golfing community which is growing rapidly. "We want to be judged in the next few years not just by the amount we have managed to increase the prize-money in what is now a far more favourable economic climate than it used to be in the mid 70s, but by the manner in which we expand," says Schofield, a man with high ideals who knows exactly where he wants the Volvo Tour to go. Having carried out a survey on their car owners, Volvo discovered that golf was a high priority in their leisure activities, and decided to switch when, for various reasons, they became disenchanted with the tennis scene. The Swedish connection pumped money into the PGA European Tour headquarters, allowing for rapid expansion when a more leisurely pace would have been necessary on the Tour's own budget, which is necessarily small as a members' organisation.

The Volvo deal was landed by the branch of the Tour known in the inner circles as simply Enterprises - a department run with slick efficiency by a former tournament administrator George O'Grady who jumped at the chance to use his earlier business skills in a totally new challenge. In the Tour Guide, O'Grady states that

Ian Woosnam celebrates another birdie (left) and Great Britain and Europe march to their famous Ryder Cup victory at The Belfry in 1985. This was the tangible fulfilment of the European dream and confirmed that the dominance of American golf had finally been broken. Above, Samuel Ryder's elegant trophy which the European team retained, for the first time on American soil, at Muirfield Village, Ohio in 1987.

the Enterprises Division has three objectives, the first being to protect and enhance the future opportunities for the Tour as a whole, largely through increasing total prize-money levels and numbers of events.

Prize levels have jumped from £1,102,220 for 23 events in 1979, to £2,411,431 for 26 events in 1983, to £5,755,137 for 26 tournaments last year. This season the prize-money is over £10 million - and will go up again in 1989. The second objective of the Enterprises Division is to increase the security of the PGA European Tour as an administrative body by improving its long term financial position, organisational structure, and operational methods; and the third is to ensure that, although marketing and endorsement agreements are made for the Tour as a whole, these, wherever possible, utilise the support of individual Tour members.

The Volvo deal envisaged the company becoming involved in sponsorship of events in various countries either directly or indirectly in a top-up capacity and this has happened and the

partnership seems to be working well. That is the biggest feather in the cap of Enterprises executive in charge O'Grady and his team.

Recently the Tour set up another two companies. One, under the control of Angel Gallardo called simply Tour South, will run what hopefully will emerge as a Spanish headquarters for the Tour in the next few years. The ambitious project envisages the development of an area for housing, and to cater for this there is now a fourth leg of the Tour operation - Tour Properties.

Initially the plan is to provide five new courses in different regions of the country - courses that will be of championship standard and capable of staging tournaments, rather like the Stadium courses built in America with the active co-operation of the US Tour. What pleased Schofield and his men about getting involved in the new project (which will have Dave Thomas, the former Ryder Cup player, as golf course designer/consultant and builder) is that it gives the Tour a chance to provide much needed new first-class facilities, not least for the young. Schofield sees this exciting venture as one which

Michael King

The striking La Manga course in Spain hosted the Spanish Open from 1973 to 1977. Now Spain is to be the centre for "Tour South" as the Tour decentralises in preparation for further advances. La Manga Club also hosts the Birchgrey Pro-Am for European clients.

The catalogue of European success continues. Sandy Lyle (right), winner of the American Masters at Augusta in 1988, and Seve Ballesteros (far right), British Open Champion 1988 at Royal Lytham and St Annes.

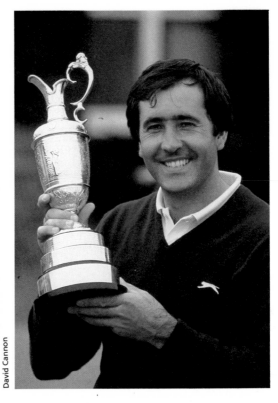

David Cannon

David Cannon

will take the Tour successfully through to the next century.

That is the commercial side but what does he see happening to the Tour on the playing side? Again Ken Schofield knows what he wants and has proved in the past that he normally gets it. Schofield is proud of the Tour and all it stands for but realises that to sustain the growth of the circuit it will be necessary to develop more opportunites for young players. Unlike America where a college golfing system provides an ideal training for a career in the profession - college golf is fiercely competitive - there is no such framework in Britain or, indeed, in Europe.

"The main tour is all-exempt," says Schofield. "and has been for some time. Technically it means that anyone with a card will be able to play in a certain number of events dependent on their ranking within the Tour. Yet we must increase the opportunities for young professionals to compete and we are channelling much of our resources and efforts with the Continentals to this end. I believe that by the end

of 1989 we will have a Second Tour Order of Merit from which a small number of golfers will qualify directly onto the main Tour."

The Tour's philosophy has always been simple enough: (1) to create opportunities for the players to play; and (2) to give them an incentive - prize-money. They have responded magnificently. Look at the catalogue of European successes around the world, not least in the majors. Severiano Ballesteros - Open Champion 1979, 1984, 1988; US Masters Champion 1981 and 1983. Sandy Lyle - Open Champion 1985 and US Masters Champion 1988. Nick Faldo - Open Champion 1987 and runner-up (beaten in a play-off) for the US Open in 1988. Bernhard Langer - US Masters Champion 1985. Ian Woosnam - winner of a record £1,000,000 in 1988 and, of course, Ryder Cup victories in 1985 and 1987 - the latter the first in the history of the match on American soil.

The system that has produced such world-beaters can continue to do so with minor refinements. For one thing the golfers today in

Top right: Estoril Golf Club, Portugal, and, bottom right, Feldafing golf course near Munich illustrate the increasing popularity of the game around Europe.

Europe play on better prepared courses than they did 20 years ago, especially on the Continent. It sometimes upsets Schofield to hear some of the top Europeans comparing the quality of tees on the American circuit with the quality of some of the greens in Europe. Richard Stilwell and his son Roger have been appointed Tour agronomists. Bruce Jamieson, head green keeper at Porthcawl, has joined the Tour to help both administratively and on the courses too.

As course conditions improve, players performances have too. You do not see players today shooting 79 to 85 unless there is a gale blowing. The battle to make the half-way cut these days is very intense. Players on the leader-board one day sometimes miss the half-way cut and that cut is seldom over par these days.

One problem which seems to persist is slow play, caused in many respects by the Tour's desire to give as many as possible of their players a game in any one week. Courses where one-tee start only is possible are particularly vulnerable to the slow round. Fines are imposed but seldom to named players. There is a feeling that everything could be speeded up were the tour to adopt the two-shot penalty for slow play. Schofield is not an advocate of the two-shot solution. He believes the fines as they are now operated impose enough of a stigma on those fined to be an adequate deterrent, but the matter is under constant review. All things considered, the Tour and its expanded commercial branch is in good heart. The problem in Europe of the banning of the South African members of the Tour, by various governments, and of those golfers of any nationality who have played in South Africa, will have to be addressed.

Ken Schofield has supervised the growth of the Tour to the point where it is more respected now than it has ever been. He is moving with confidence into a new decade of expansion on many more fronts. It is as exciting now for him and his team as it was when he first joined the Tour in the early 70s. Much has been achieved. Much more will be as the Tour expands in Spain and the game grows in popularity in Sweden, France, Italy, Switzerland, Portugal, Germany, Holland and even Morocco. The Panasonic European Open is glad to be part of the vibrant scene.

Index